A Candle in the Dark:

or,

A Treatise Concerning the Nature of Witches and Witchcraft:

Being Advice to Judges, Sheriffes, Justices of the Peace, and Grand-Jury-men,

what to do, before they passe Sentence on such as are Arraigned for their Lives as Witches.

A Candle in the Dark:

OR, A TREATISE

Concerning the Nature of Witches and Witchcraft:

BEING

Advice to Judges Sheriffes, Justices of the Peace and Grand-Jury-
men, what to do, before they passe Sentence on such as are
Arraigned for their Lives, as WITCHES.

By THOMAS ADY, M.A.

1656.

The Reason of the Book.

The Grand Errour of these latter Ages is ascribing power to Witches, and by foolish imagination of mens brains, without grounds in the Scriptures, wrongfull killing of the innocent under the name of Witches; unto which Idolatry and bloud-guiltiness (being as bad, or worse than the Idolatry of the ancient Heathen) men are led as violently by fond imagination, as were the Ephesians to the worshipping of Diana, and of the Image which (as they blindly thought) fell down from Jupiter, Acts 19. 35. It is reported by Travellers, that some People in America do worship, for a day, the first living Creature they see in the morning, be it but a Bird, or a Worm; this Idolatry is like the Idolatry of this part of the World, who when they are afflicted in Body, or Goods, by Gods hand, they have an eye to some Mouse, or Bugg, or Frog, or other living Creature, saying, It is some Witches Impe that is sent to afflict them, ascribing the Work of God, to a Witch, or any mean Creature rather than to God.

Mr. Scot published a Book, called his Discovery of Witchcraft, in the beginning of the Reign of Queen Elizabeth, for the instruction of all Judges, and Justices of those times; which Book did for a time take great impression in the Magistracy, and also in the Clergy, but since that time England hath shamefully fallen from the Truth which they began to receive; wherefore here is again a necessary and illustrious discourse for the Magistracy, and other People of this Age, where I intreat all to take notice, that many do falsly report of Mr. Scot, that he held an Opinion, that Witches are not, for it was neither his Tenent, neither is it mine; but that Witches are not.

The First Book, shewing what Witches are in the Scripturesence, throughout the Old and New Testament.

The Second Book, shewing how grosly the Scriptures have been mis-interpreted by Antichrist concerning Witches, by which interpretation he hath made the Nations go astray. With a confutation of those Errours.

The Third Book, touching some erroneous English Writers, who have upheld the same Errours which Antichrist hath broached to the world; Also the Works of a Scotch-man, called, The Works of King James. With an addition of fifteen Causes; also a reference to Scot, and also the opinion of Luther concerning Devils. Also an instruction to Lawyers.

Dedication

TO THE Prince of the Kings of the Earth. IT is the manner of men, O heavenly King, to dedicate their Books to some great men, thereby to have their Works protected and countenanced among men; but thou only art able by thy holy Spirit of Truth to defend thy Truth, and to make it take impression in the heart and understanding of men: Unto thee alone do I dedicate this Work, intreating thy most High Majesty to grant, That whoever shall open this Book, thy holy Spirit may so possess their understanding, as that the spirit of errour may depart from them, and that they may read, and try thy Truth by the touchstone of thy Truth, the holy Scriptures, and finding that Truth may embrace it, and forsake these darksome inventions of Antichrist, that have deluded and defiled the Nations now, and in former Ages. Enlighten the World, thou that art the Light of the World, and let Darkness be no more in the World now, or in any future Age; but make all people to walk as Children of the Light for ever; and destroy Antichrist that hath deceived the Nations, and save us the residue, by thy self alone, and let not Satan any more delude us; for the Truth is thine for ever.

B

To the Reader

To the Reader. SIR, IF you be a courteous Reader, I intreat you that what weaknesse and imperfections you shall think you espie in this Book from the Author thereof, you passe them by for the Truths sake whereupon this Book treateth. Secondly, if you be so discourteous as to carp and censure, then I intreat you to carp only at me, and not at the Truth, lest you resist the truth. Thirdly,. I intreat you to Read my Book thorow before you cast it by, for otherwise, Sir, it may argue weaknesse in yourself to slight the Book before you see the Argument. It is one of the vanities of the World to write many Books, and when a man hath taken pains to write, few men will take the pains to read; which Solomon intimateth Eccle. 12. 12. but Sir, if you find no leasure to read and consider, then I pray find no leasure to gainsay, or to argue against. Fourthly, for all places of Scripture alledged in this Book, if you shall search our English Translations, and not find them to carry the sense which I drive at in my discourse, I intreat you either to search the Originall, or else to look upon the Latin Translations of Junius and Tremellius, which carry the true sense of the Originall, as it was written by the Spirit of God.

Your Friend T. A.

Non quis, sed quid.

To the Clergie of England

To the more Judicious and Wise, and Dis- creet part of the Clergie of ENGLAND. Joshua 7. 11. THese words, Israel hath sinned, are not so to be understood, as if Israel had been free from all other sins but only that of Achan, and yet that sinne of Achan was the sinne that kindled the anger of God against Israel; so likewise, 2 Sam. 21. 1. David had been an adulterer, Joab was a murderer, Shimei a rayler, Sheba a wicked man of Belial, and many sins were in Israel at that time, and yet the sinne that kindled Gods wrath, and brought the famine, was the blood-guiltiness of Saul, as appeareth in the Chapter and verse aforesaid; so likewise 1 Kings 16. 30. Ahab was more wicked than all that were before him, yet the sin that cost him his life, and his crown, was murthering of Naboth, Chapter 21. 19. so that it is easily gathered, that some one abominable sinne doth sometimes more provoke God to anger, against any particular man, or against a Nation, than all other sinnes that are commonly committed. Then you that should be as messengers from God, in that you cry against sinne in generall, yee do well, but in that yee seek not out this cursed Achans wedg that hath defiled England and the Christian world, look to it betimes, lest it be laid to your charge, if the Nations perish for lack of knowledg.

Your Friend T. A.

Non quis, sed quid.

B

Preface

Since the time that I have tryed to bring truth upon the stage of the world, to be censured by all men, I being acquainted with but few in comparison of all, and some of them knowing my intent to put this discourse in Print, I have nearly guessed by common discourse amongst them, what the censure of this book will be, that is, it will be the same among many, that it is among few; for among few, I find some so reasonable in their discourse, that when they find by argumentation, that there is reason and grounds in the Scripture for what I write, they upon second cogitations, and deliberate musings, have yeelded to this truth, (and some of them very learned.) Some again, after some serious argumentation, being fully convinced that this is the very truth, yet doe still suspend their censure, till they see how it will be approved of by others; by which they shew they are ready at all times, to beleeve as the Church beleeves, and to pin their opinion upon the sleeve of other mens judgements. A third sort there are, who at the first onset of discourse, do think themselves so surely grounded, and this truth so groundlesse and vain an opinion, as that they cannot speak without disdain, as great. Goliah spake to little David, and thus they beginne in fury, O grosse! what madnesse is this? what will you deny the Scriptures? what answer you to this? Thou shalt not suffer a Witch to live: but when they are so suddenly answered, and suddenly convinced, that this place of Scripture maketh nothing for them, and that this their great Champion-argument, hath so soon received a stone in the forehead, they either let their discourse fall to the ground like Goliah, and slight this as a new opinion; or else they runne away cowardly, like the host of the Philistines, and forsake the Scriptures (which they first pretended should be their only weapon to fight withall) and betake themselves to their leggs, runing into some vain story taken out of Bodinus or Bat. Spineus, or some such popish vain writer, and report that it was done in Lancashier, or in Westmerland, or in some remote place farre off; and that they heard it credibly reported from men of worth and quality, and so they ingage me to answer to a story, which they would compell me to beleeve, or else to goe see where it was done; but if it happeneth (as often it doth, that I make it appear by Scripture, that it is absurd or impossible, not to be reported by a Christian, or that I shew them the story, in any of the afore said Authers, who have been the Authors of many vain fables, then they presently fly to another story, as vain and absurd as the former, and that being answered, they fly to another, saying, Sir, what do you answer to this? in which manner of disputes I have heard sometimes such monstrous impossibilities reported and affirmed to be true, (for they had it by credible report) as would make the Angells in Heaven blush to hear them. Therefore setting aside all such unscholar-like way of arguing, I desire all to argue by the Scriptures, and I will answer, or to answer by the Scriptures, and I will argue by the Scriptures, as followeth in this Dilemma.

B

A Dilemma that Cannot bee
answered by Witch-Mongers

Luke 4. 4, 8, 12. Christ who is our forerunner, Heb. 6. 20. by whofe holy Spirit the holy Scriptures were written, whose words were of equall truth and authority with the Scriptures; Yet when he was to conquer the father of lies, the Prince of darknesse (not for his own sake, but for our example) although hee was able to have argued by common reason, beyond the wisedome of Solomon, yet being tempted, would not answer any one temptation without Scriptum est, it is written (because the Scriptures are the only rule of righteousnesse;) whosoever then will take example by him, to try the Truth by Scriptures, and to argue by them, as he did in this place of Luke, (and not by strange reports, which are the objects of vain credulity) let them answer me by Scriptum est.

1 Where is it written in all the old and new Testament, that a Witch is a murtherer, or hath power to kill by Witchcraft, or to afflict with any disease or infirmity?

2 Where is it written, that Witches have Imps sucking of their bodies?

3 Where is it written, that Witches have biggs for Imps to suck on?

4 Where is it written, that the Devill setteth privy marks upon Witches, whereby they should be known or searched out? or that any man or woman hath any mark upon their body any more than natural, or by some disease or hurt, which is preternatural?

5 Where is it written, that the tryall of a Witch should be by sinking or swimming in the water? or by biggs or privy marks, or suspition of people, to be signes of a Witch?

6 Where is it written, that Witches can hurt corn or cattell, or transport corn by Witchcraft, or can fly in the aire, and do many such strange wonders?

7 Where is it written, that a Witch is such a man or woman that maketh a league with the Devill, written with his or her

blood, and by vertue of that covenant to have the Devill at command?

8 Where is it written, that any man or woman was called in the Scripture strix, or lamia, or where is any word of such signification or importance, either in the Hebrew text, or in the Latin translation, where is a Witch said in the Scriptures to be any such kind of person?

9 What is a witch in the scripture sense, according to Deu.18.10,11 where all sorts of witches are nominated by nine terms of description?

10 Where is it written, that there are any other sorts of Witches than such as are there described? Deut.18.10,11.

11 Where do we read of a he devill, or a she devill, called incubus or succubus, that useth generation or copulation with Witches, or Witches with them?

12 It is written, Woe unto such as devour widdows houses, and in a pretence make long prayers, Matth.23.14.

13 It is written, the Lord hateth the hand that sheddeth innocent blood, and the fals witness that speaketh lies, and the feet that are swift to do mischeif, and a heart that deviseth wicked imaginations, Pro.6.17 18,19.

14 It is written, shall there be evill in a City and the Lord hath not done it? Amos..3.6.

15 It is written, there is no God with me, I kill and I make alive; I wound, and heal, Deut.32.39. and again, the Lord killeth, and maketh alive; hee bringeth down to the grave, and bringeth up; the Lord maketh poore, and maketh rich, I Sam. 2,6,7.

16 It is written, If ye were blind yee had had no sinne, but now ye say ye see, therefore your sinne remaineth, John 9.41.

17 It is written, Because they received not the love of the Truth, that they might be saved; therefore God shall send them strong delusions, that they should beleeve lies, that they might be damned that beleeved not the Truth, but had pleasure in unrighteousness 2 Thes.2.10,11,12.

18 It is written, Thou shalt not raise a false report: put not thy hand with the wicked to be an unrighteous witnesse, Exodus 23.1.

19 It is written, If ye any way afflict the widdow or the fatherlesse, and they cry at all unto me, I will surely hear their cry; and my wrath shal wax hot, and I will kill you with the sword, and your wives shall be widdows, and your children fatherlesse, Exodus 22.23,24.

20 It is written, God saw that the imaginations of the thoughts of mens hearts were only evill continually; and it repented the Lord that he had made man, and therefore he destroyed the old world, Gen. 6.5,6,7, Therefore you that are of the sacred order of the ministry; that do use to cry to the people, give ear with fear and reverence to the word of God, as it is written in the text, how dare ye teach for doctrin, the traditions of Antichrist that are not written in the Book of God? Whether do not some preferre the mad imaginations of Cornelius Agrippa and others, before the Scriptures, for the defending their opinions?

So much for my Dilemma, now for the Text.

The First Book

A Candle in the Dark: SHEWING The Divine Cause of the distractions of the whole Nation of ENGLAND, and of the Christian World.

Deuteronomy 18. 10,11. LEt the Reader take notice that in all the Scriptures there is not any kind of Witch spoken of but such as are mentioned in these two verses; which that every one may understand, I will expound punctually, not according to our English obscure-translations, but according to the true meaning, and signification of the originall text, as it was written by Moses in the Hebrew tongue, and as it is truely translated (for the better and easier satisfaction of many that have not knowledge in the Hebrew tongue;) by Junius, and Tremellius, in their Latin Bible; whether also I referre the Reader for all places of Scripture, alledged in this Book; and here I do in Gods name, and in Zeal for his truth, desire and intreat him that thinketh himself the learnedst Clerk, to shew mee in all the Scriptures, such a word as Striges or lamiae, or any word of that signification, importing such doctrins, as have a long time defiled the Nations. Deut. 18. 10, 11. Let there not be found among you, any that maketh his sonne or his daughter to passe thorow the fire, a user of divinations, a planetarian, or a Conjecturer, or a Jugler. Also a user of charmes, or one that seeketh an Oracle, or a South-sayer, or one that asketh counsell of the dead. The Latin translation is this. Ne invenitor in te quitraducat filium suum, aut filiam suam per ignem, utens divinationibus, planetarius, aut conjector, aut præstigiator, Item utens incantatione, aut requirens prthonem, aut ariolus, aut necromantis;

And here is the Hebrew Text written in the Roman character, with the construction, of every word. Lo jimatzæ ne invenitor, beca in te, magnabir quitraducat, beno filium suum, uubitto aut filigm suam, baese per ignem, kosem kesamim divinans divinationes, megnonen, planearius, uumenachese aut conjector, umechascscph aut præstigiator, vechobhir chabher incantans incantatione, vessoel ob requirens pythonem, vejiddegnoni, aut ariolus, vedhorese el hamethim aut consulens mortuos; so much for the Text. Exodus. 22. 18. Mechascscepha le thechajek, præstigiatricem non fines vivere.

There is also another word, Hartumim in Exodus 4. 17. Gen. 41 8. and in other places, which is taken in the generall sense for Magnus a Magician; that hath one or all these crafts or impostures, yet by many it is restrained to the particular, and often translated Ariolus, being the most allowed signification, for Arioli, were called Magi, being counted wise men, and therefore the word is used for all sorts of Magicians; these and all other words in the Scriptures concerning Witches are consonant to the words in the Text. The Text opened.

The Text is verbatim, according to the Originall as it was written by Moses in the Hebrew tongue, which I will expound orderly: and here is to be noted, that in these two verses, are nine sorts of Witches nominated by God, unto Moses, and the people, to this end and purpose; that whereas God hath chosen the people of Israel, to be a peculiar church and people to himself, he would be their only Counsellor, to keep them in the way of wisdome and holinesse, and therefore commandeth them, in no wise to aske counsell of any but the true prophets and messengers of God, as appeareth in the 14. and 15. verses of this chapter, and because there were so many sorts of people in the world, that did commonly abuse and usurp the office of Gods Prophets: God describeth them, in the 10. and 11. verses of this chapter, by nine severall nominations or descriptions, commanding them to shun and avoyd them as false Prophets and deceivers of the people; for it was the manner of the heathen (to seek unto such for counsell,) and the Lord having cast out those heathen people, for such abominable ways giveth his own people warning of all such ways to avoid them, and not to hearken to them namely, to those nine sorts of witches, or deceivers, or false prophets, or seducers of the people from God and his prophets, to lying Idolatrous waies, and giveth them warning in the three last verses of the same chapter of all false Prophets whatsoever, that should presumptuously take upon them to speak any thing in Gods name which God had not commanded, or to speak in the name of other Gods, that such should be slain, and these nine appellations in the tenth and eleventh verses, are not tearms of distinction, but several terms of description, whereby to discern false Prophets, or Witches, whom the Lord would have cut off from among his people; and therefore the Lord describeth them in the tenth and eleventh verses, sheweth the destruction of the Nations that hearkened to them, in the 12, 13, and 14. verses (where also he commandeth his people to be holy, and not like those Nations) promiseth that his people should always have a true Prophet amongst them to hearken unto, in the 15, 16, 17, and 18. verses (which although it was fulfilled in Christ chiefly, Acts 3. 23. yet it is meant, and also verified of all the rest of the Prophets, that were successively Messengers of Christ from Moses, till the coming of Christ in the Flesh) commandeth them to hearken to such a Prophet, in the nineteenth verse, but for all false Prophets, the Lord will have them cut off in the twentieth verse, and setteth down a trial, and a discerning rule between a true Prophet, and a false Prophet that speaketh in Gods Name, in the one and twentieth and two and twentieth verses, as appeareth orderly in the chapter, who so pleaseth to read it. And now to come to the Exposition, or Interpretation of these two verses, Deut. 18. 10, 11. and of the nine appellations or descriptions therein contained. And first, for the first. Let there not be found among you, any that maketh his Son or his Daughter to pass through the fire, this is the first description whereby God describeth a Witch, or a false Prophet; and in what manner this should be a description of a Witch, or false Prophet, that we may the better understand, I must first define what a Witch is, and then come to the matter. The Definition of a Witch, or a certain Demonstration what a Witch is (for the vulgar capacity.) A Witch is a Man, or Woman, that practiseth Devillish crafts, of seducing the people for gain, from the knowledge and worship of God, and from the truth to vain credulity (or beleeving of lyes) or to the worshipping of Idols. So likewise for the definition of Witchcraft. WItchcraft is a devillish

21

Craft of seducing the people for gain, from the knowledge and worship of God, and from his Truth to vain credulity (or beleeving of lyes) or to the worshipping of Idols. That it is a Craft truly so called, and likewise that it is for gain is proved, Act. 16.16.19. the Maid that followed Paul crying, brought in her Master much gain; And that it is a Craft of perverting the people, or seducing them from God and his Truth, is proved, Acts 13.6,7,8. Elimas the Sorcerer laboured to pervert the Deputy from the Faith, So likewise, Acts 8.9,10,11.verses, it doth more plainly prove all in these words, And there was a man before in the City called Simon, which used Witchcraft, and bewitched the people of Samaria, saying, That he himself was some great man, to whom they gave heed from the least to the greatest, saying, This man is the great power of God, and gave heed unto him, because that of long time hee had bewitched them with Sorceries; How bewitched them with Sorceries? That is, seduced them with devillish Crafts (as the Greek, and also Tremtlius Latine Translation do more plainly illustrate) in this sense speaketh Paul to the Galathians, 3. 1. O foolish Galathians, Who hath bewitched you, that you should not obey the truth? And that a Witch, or Witchcraft is taken in no other sense in all the Scripture, it appeareth by the whole current of the Scriptures, as you may fee in this Book. But now to return to the Text. Deut. 18.10,11. THe first description of a Witch in the Text is, Let there not be found among you, any that maketh his San, on his Daughter to pass through the fire. Here we must note that there was in those dayes a great Idol of great request-among the Heathen, the name of which Idol was Molech, and was first set up by the Ammonites, I King.11.5 and by them called Milcom, and from thence grew in request, and defiled a great part of the world, who was generally led after it to Idolatry, insomuch that the Kings and Nobles of the earth did sometimes make their Sons and their Daughters pass through the fire in honour to that Idol, as Manasses did, 2 Chron.33.6. and how that passing through the fire, was, or in what manner, is questionable: Some think they burnt them in the fire, as Burnt-offerings to that Idol, because it is said, Deut. 12. 21. they burnt their Sons and their Daughters in the fire to their gods: And also in Psal.106.38. And 2 Chron. 28.3. Abaz burnt his children in the fire, and c. But although some Historians do report that the heathen did sometimes (upon some extraordinary request made to their Idol) consume their children as a Burnt-sacrifice. Which might seem to some so to bee understood in these places of Scripture, yet if we compare one place of Scripture with another (where burning and passing through the fire are used as termes equivalent) upon the same subject) we may see that burning is not taken in that sense, to consume them in the fire, for then they had bereaved themselves of children; But Manasses and Ahaz were not left childless, for their sons reigned in their stead, but burning is by a Metalepsis taken for passing through the fire, that is, they made them pass through the fire as an Idolatrous ceremony, whereby they dedicated them to their Idol, as in 2 King. 23. 10. This exposition is most allowable, but yet (not tying any man to this exposition) I say, that in what manner soever it was that they made their children to pass through the fire, the scope and meaning of the text, Dent.18.10. is, That they should not bee Ringleaders to Idolatry, as in Levit. 20. 5. whosoever did give his children to Molech was to bee slain, with all that followed him in his Idolatry, they that followed him to Idolatry were to bee slain as Idolaters, but hee that gave his children to Molech, to make them pass through the fire, is chiefly named here to be slain, as a Ring-leader of other men to Idolatry, and is in Deut.18.10. reckoned amongst Witches, according to the definition of a Witch afore-shewed, Witches being in all the Scripture-sense only seducers or inticers of the people to spiritual Whoredom, and here in the text Moses speaketh, per Synecdochen, of one Idol for all; all one as if he had said, Let none be found among you that is an inticer or ring-leader of the people to Idolatry, in which sence all Idol Priests are Witches, and are stiled so in common Scripture phrase, 1 Sam. 6. 2. the Philistims called their Priests, and South-sayers together; for the setting up or upholding of any Idol, is the Grand Witch-craft of all, and the very Mother of all other Witch-craft, and it is most probable the Priests of Molech were first devoted to that service, by using that Ceremony of passing through the fire; and all that did in like manner pass through the fire did become Priests, or at least Servants to the Idol, for the work of the Burnt-offerings, in this sence is Jesabel, called a Witch, 2 King.9.22. Why was it said the Witch-crafts of Jesabel? Because shee was an upholder of Baal, and his Prophets, who were jugling Seducers of the people to Idolatry: Why in the same verse is it said the Whoredoms of Jesabel? Because Spiritual Whoredom (or Idolatry) and Witch-craft are inseparable companions, therefore it is said, Scortationes and prestigia Jezebela, the Whoredoms, and juglings, or Witch-crafts of Jesabel; in this sence is Manasses truly said to use Witchcraft, Chron. 33. and the first eight verses, almost all that is spoken of in Deut. 18. 10, 11. Manasses is said to be guilty of in this place of Chronicles; First, he set up several Idols, and immediatly follows the inseparable companions, that is the Witches, or Priests of Idols, called here South-sayers, with their several Witch-crafts, in the sixth verse of the same Chapter of the Chronicles. Why do Idols, and Witch-crafts, and Witches come in rolling together so thick in this place? The first Reason is, because as the setting up of an Idol is Witch-craft, so where Idols are, there must needs bee Witches; namely South-sayers, or Idol Priests, or else the Idol of itself can do nothing; as when it is said in 2 King. 1, 2. Ahaziah sent to inquire of the god of Ekron, it is not to be supposed that there could be an answer given by the bare Idol (being but a stock) but the answer or Divination must come from the Priests and South-sayers, that were there belonging to that Idol, and upholding it. The second Reason is, because as I have said before of the nine several appellations of Witches in Deut. 18. 10, 11, that they are not terms of distinction but of description; so here in the 2 Chron. 33. all that is said of Manasses in the seven first Verses of the Chapter, is not to be understood as expressions of several distinct things done by Manasses, but a full expression of one thing by several terms of description, expressing fully that one act of Manasses, that is, first he set up several Idols, as in the third, fourth, and fifth, and the beginning of the sixt verse of the Chapter doth appear; and then it followeth that he used those things that did necessarily belong to the Idol, without which the Idol could be of no force, or request among the people, and that was as appeareth in the sixth verse, he used Divinations, and Conjecturings, and Juglings, and set up an Oracle, and Southsayers, (the Latine translation is) Et divinationibus, and conjectationibus, and prestigiis usus est, instituitq; pythonem and ariolos) so all that Manasses did, was setting up of Idols with their adjuncts, and though the Idols indeed were several and various, yet all was one act, tending only to the making up of one compleat Idol-house, that was the House of God, verse the fourth, and seventh, he abusing it, and making it an House of Idols, this one act produced one effect; that was, he made Judah and Jerusalem go astray to Idolatry, as appeareth verse nine, but Josiah destroyed the Idols, with their Adjuncts, Oracles, and South-sayers, 2 King. 23, 24. being Idol Priests. So much for the first and grand description of a Witch in the text, that is, a Ring-leader to Idolatry, intimated in these words, Let there not be found among you, any that maketh his son or his Daughter to pass through the fire; this first description being rightly understood, the other eight will bee the more easily expounded, being but appurtenances to the first, or rather Monsters in the belly of the first. Now followeth the second description, or appellation of a Witch, that is, Let there not be found among you, any that isseth Divinations. To use Divinations was to take upon them to tell things to come, and things hidden, which things could not be done by any but by God, and his Prophets, as appeareth, Isa. 41. 23. Shew what is to come after, that we may know that yee are gods; yet as Gods Prophets could tell things to come, so in the second of Kings, 6. 12. Elisha the Prophet could tell the King of Israel what was spoken in the secret Chamber of the King of Aram; and although God would have his people know, that none could do these things truly but himself, by his Prophets, and therefore hee would have his people to hearken after none but his Prophets, in enquiring of things to come, or things hidden; yet many false Prophets did take upon them to tell such things meerly to seduce the people for gain, pretending that they could do it, either by vertue of their Idol, and so led the people a whoring after them, as in 2 King. I. 2. Ahaziah sent to enquire of the god of Ekron, and Jeremiah, 23. 13. they Prophesied by Beal, and seduced my people. Or else falsly pretending themselves to be Gods Prophets, and so in a fair pretence, to pervert the people from the truth to lyes, as Micha 3. 11. Quorum Propheta, pecunia divinant, whose Prophets do give Divinations for money; and Jer. 23. 21. I have not spoken to them, and yet they have Prophesied saith the Lord. In this sence Samuel said to Saul, Rebellio est sicut peccatum divinationis, Rebellion is as the sin of divination, or according to our English translations, is as the sin of Witch-craft, I Sam, 15. 23. and for these divinations, and false Prophesies they had this colour, That whereas God did usually speak to his Prophets in Dreams, and Visions of the night, as appeareth, Numb. 12. 6. these Witches, or false Prophets pretended that they had also Dreamed, and had seen Visions, that so they might bewitch and seduce the people from Gods way, Deut. 13. I. 5. and also Jer. 23. 25. They prophesie lyes in my name, saying, I have dreamed, I. have dreamed; and vers. 27. Think they to cause my people so to forget my Name by their Dreams, which they tell every one to his neighbour, as their father s have for gotten my name for Baal? not but that Dreams were to be declared and regarded, if it were truly done without deceit, for it followeth in the twenty eighth verse, He that hath a Dream, let him tell a dream, and he that hath my Word, let-him speak my Word faithfully; but these Dreamers, or Witches, did falsly pretend Dreams and Visions, that they might seduce the people, vers, 32. these were the right Enthusiasts of the Heathen, this was one great practise of the Priests of the great Idol Apollo, that was called the Oracle of Apollo, they would lye down behind the Altar, and sleep for a time, and then make people beleeve they had seen a Vision, whereby they could determine their matters, and accordingly gave their Divinations, or Oracles; many other colours, or pretences, had their Diviners, for their cheating Witch-craft, or Divinations, as they would make the people beleeve they could talk with the spirit departed of the dead, and so know things hidden, or things to come, but of that more in the ninth description, and indeed most of the following descriptions, or appellations in the text were linken to the second, to lying Divinations, as also linked to each other, yet because the manner of their actions were various, the Lord here describeth them according to the variety of their actions, all tending to one end, and that is to oppose the way of God, and the Prophets for gain.

A Question resolved.

Seeing it is manifest by the Scriptures, as appeareth in this second description of a Witch, that he that useth Divinations is a Witch, and one main prerence in giving Divinations, was Dreams and Visions of the night, then it may bee supposed that he that telleth a Dream to his neighbour, there-by fore-telling things to come, useth Divinations, and ought to bee censured as a Witch, or else must needs bee a Prophet. To this it is answered, That Dreams in the Scripture do appear to be of two sorts, the first sort were Prophetical, wherein men had a direct command from God to go and Prophesie to the people, and these Dreams came ordinarily to the Prophets, upon so many several occasions as were needful for the Prophets to admonish the people, to shew them their sins, and declare the truth to them, and for the declaring of future things to the people, either concerning Judgments of God that would come upon them for their sins if they did not amend, or concerning some great work, that God would do for his people that feared him, and these Dreams were proper to the Prophets only, Numb. 12.6. and they that did falsly pretend such Dreams, and Inspirations, to dissemble the Prophets, to seduce the people to Idolatry were Witches, or false Prophets, according to this second description of using lying Divinations, and ought to bee slain, Deut. 13.1.5.

Secondly, the second sort of Dreams that we read of in the Scriptures were warning Dreams, whereby men were forewarned of things to come, but were not thereby sent to Prophesie to the people by special command from God, but were forewarned; First, for the avoyding of danger that might come upon them, or others whom this Dream concerned, or at the least that they might know the danger before it came, and these Dreams were common to many as well as to the Prophets, both to the godly and ungodly, Mat. 2.12, 13 and 27.19. Gen. 40.8.and Chap.41.Dan. 2.1. Secondly, these sort of warning Dreams fore-shewed a blessing upon the godly to encourage them, Gen. 37.5.9. and for these sorts of Dreams, we read by these examples in the Scriptures, that they are common to all sorts of people, and useful either to hear, or to declare, but whosoever did declare a Prophetical Dream, was either a true Prophet indeed, or else a lying Enthusiast, or false Prophet (such as were the Idol Priests of the Heathen) to seduce the people, as is shewed in the Scriptures before mentioned in this second description, and also in Jeremiah 23.16.25. And whereas some may question whether Dreams are now sent by God to forewarn, as in ancient times, so long as we have no Scripture to the contrary (but rather for it) wee may not deny it; and do also finde by common experience that some have dreamed of their Childe falling into the fire, and some into the water, and of other several dangers concerning themselves, and others, of which some have come to pass that might have been prevented, by prayer and diligent care. I know a man that was fore-warned in a Dream of these Wars in England before they began, (or were like to bee) but Prophetical Dreams are not usual in these days. Yet here it may further be noted, that in some case a man may also declare a Prophetical Dream, and yet be neither a true Prophet, nor a Witch, or false Prophet; and that hath sometimes been seen by experience in such as have been troubled in their phantasies through distemper of body, or other distracting occasions hurting their phantasie, they imagine that God hath spoken to them by Dream, or Vision, or Voyce heard, or by an Angel, and hath bidden them go Prophesie such and such things, and these are to be charitably judged of, and not rashly censured; this distemper of body may be discerned by the effects, that is, Death, or Sickness following within a short time after, if not prevented by the Phisitians; also troubled phansie by outward distractions may be discerned by the fore-going occasions that have troubled them, and hurt their phansies; and here is required great discretion in all that shall see, or hear a Man or Woman declare a Message from God (as he thinketh) for the intent of a false Prophet is only to deceive, or seduce for advantage of gain or preferment; some have written concerning Dreams, that some Dreams are Diabolical, which are only Philosophical Notions, having no grounds in the Scripture. And whereas it is manifest in the Scriptures that God speaketh to men by Dreams, and interpretations of Dreams are only by the Spirit of God, Gen. 40.8 I think it presumption and Phantasie, to adde any such distinction of Dreams, except Enthusiasmes, which although they are of the Devil, yet are no real Dreams, but Lyes, for the Enthusiasts did falsly pretend that they had Dreamed, Jer. 23.25.27.32. Natural Dreams I deny not, which come from the multitude of business, and from the natural disposition of the body, but none of these are any way concerning future events, but are only the objects of our Natural affections, and although some of these are lascivious Dreams, some Murtherous some Covetous, and in that sence may be called Diabolical; yet in these Dreams are nothing besides Nature, neither hath the Devil any further act in them than in our corrupt stragling affections in the day time; and though our thoughts are sometimes worse in the night than in the day, it is because our affections are busied in the day with other objects preventing such thoughts. So much for the Second description of a Witch in the text, that is an user of Divinations or false Prophesies.

The Third Description.

The Third description of a Witch in the text, Deut. 18.10, 11. is Planetarus, let there not be found among you a Planetarian;

some have thought by a Planetarian here is meant such a one as did observe the course and influence of the Planets, and from thence gave predictions of future events, that these were unlawful Arts, and ought not to be practised, and therefore have absolutely condemned judiciall Astrology, but if they be right in this opinion, how then do they answer to Psal. 19.1. The Firmament sheweth the works of his hands; this is not to be understood only of the making of the Canopy of Heaven, for then it had been said the Firmament is the works of his hands (he that liketh not this exposition, let him read Cornelius Gemma de natura Cometæ) and God himself speaketh of the influence of the Heavens, Job 38.31. Canst thou restrain the sweet influence of the Pleiades, or canst thou loose the bonds of Orion? and c. And whereas some have said, That the Star that shewed the birth of Christ, Mat. 2. 2. was Miraculous, and not any Natural Star, how then could the Wise men or Astrologians see the signification of that Star by their Science of Astrologie, whereas if it reacheth not to the knowledge of future contingensies, then much less to the knowledge of things supernatural or miraculous, and yet they saw that the Stars appearance did signifie the birth of that great King (although I deny not, that the motion of the star in the ninth verse might bee miraculous.) And to come farther, Judg.5.20. the Stars in their Rampires fought against Sisera; it is not spoken of any thing beyond nature, but the Prophets did observe that the stars in their natural places fought against Sisera, also Gen. 1. 14. God made the Lights of Heaven to be signs for seasons, and for days, and for years; it seemeth then that judicial Astrology is not condemned in the Scripture, if it be not abused; what then was a Planetarian in the sence of the text? and why were they forbidden by God, and set in the Catalogue of Witches? To this it is answered, That under the colour of Astrologie these Planetarians that are here forbidden did harbour themselves, that because there was somewhat in that Science for the knowledge of some future things, therefore in the pretence of their knowledge in that Science they did take upon them to compare themselves with the Prophets, and to draw the people after their uncertain

Predictions, as if they had been equal with the Prophets, and many of them having no knowledge at all in that Science, yet did under the colour there of harbour their deceitful Oracles, or Divinations, ascribing a Deity to the Planets, calling them gods, as Mars the god of Warre, Venus the goddess of Beauty, and c. and did also ascribe so much to their influence, as they beleeved no power above them, and so drew the people a whoring after them, to make them forget God the Author of all things, and to Deifie the Creature; and these Planetarians being meer Naturalists, and beleeving no power above the Planets, would bear a breast against the Prophets, and undertake to do those things that were only proper to the Prophets to do, and could be done by no other power but by the Spirit of God, Dan. 2. 2, 3, 4. they would undertake the interpretation of Dreams, if the dreams were related to them, nevertheless the expounding of dreams is of God only, vers. 27.28. and Gen. 41. 16. and 40. 8. And whereas God did put into the heart of Nebuchadnezzar, to put them to difficult task, they said no man upon earth was able to do it, Dan. 2.10. inferring that the Prophets themselves could do no more than they; yea so did they deifie the Planets, that they ascribed to them to be the gods of the seven Days of the Week, and caused the people to worship them, and bring their daily oblations to them, and to keep Holy days to them, from the names of which Planets the days do take their nominations; as Sunday from the Sun, Monday from the Moon, and c. and in other Tongues is more manifest for every day; which if it be true that the Planets have their several influences upon the several days of the Week, yet their wickedness was in denying God that made the Heavens, and their Host, and in deifying the Creature; and for this they are described among Witches, or seducers of the people to Idolatry, and this Idolatry God warneth his people to avoyd, Deut. 4. 19. Take heed when thou liftest up thine eyes to Heaven, and seest the Sun, and the Moon, and Stars, with all the Host of Heaven, shouldest be driven to worship them and serve them, which the Lord thy God hath distributed to all people under heaven. Although God had given and distributed their influence to all people under Heaven, yet men may not worship them, but worship God that made them. So likewise Deut. 17. 3. also this Idolatry part of the Israelites were defiled with, Jer. 44 17. they burnt Incense, and poured Drink-offerings to the Queen of Heaven, or (as it is in the Original) to the works of Heaven, that is, to the Planets; of this Idolatry Job cleareth himself, Job 31. 26. If I did behold the Sun when it shined, or the Moon walking in her brightness (that is, if I did behold them with adoration) this had been iniquity, for I had denied the God above, as followeth vers. 28. also 2 Chron. 33. 5. This was part of Manasses Witchcraft, he built Altars to all the Hoft of Heaven, and made the people go astray, vers. 9. And so for this Third description of a Witch in the text, a Planetarian, that is, that under the colour of Astrologie seduceth the people to lying vanities, or Divinations, and causeth them to deifie and Idolize the Planets, or that boasteth himself in his Predictions against the Prophets, crying peace when the Prophets Prophesie destruction, Isa. 47. 13. Let thy Astrologians stand up that do view the Stars, and do make known their monthly Predictions, and save thee from the things that shall come upon thee. I might quote also some prophane Writers of this sort, who are seducing Witches, because under pretence of Astrologie they teach things beyond the intent and scope of that, or any lawful Science. As Julius Maternus hath devillishly written, That he that is born when Saturn is in Leone, shall live long, and go to Heaven when he dyeth; and so Albumazar saith, Who so prayeth to God when the Moon is in Capite draconis, shall obtain his prayer. These Planetarians, for these and the like impious devices, in pretence of a lawful Science, are described in the text among Witches. Astrologians have also annexed to their Science of Astrologie, Palmistrie, and Physiognomie, the Cælestial Bodies, as they say, having fixed their Characters upon the inferiour Bodies of men (as he that readeth their Books may fee, with the reason thereof) and therefore these Arts together with Astrologie do serve them to make their Prognosticks concerning the strength, health, disposition, and several events of any mans life; which Prognosticks do often happen true, because Natures course may be probably conjectured by the course and character of the Planets (although these Arts are much abused by wandring Gypsies, who under colour of such knowledge, do commonly cheat silly people, and also rob their pockets, when they are viewing their hands and face to tell them their Fortunes;) now herein was one difference between Planetarians, or Astrologians, lawful or unlawful in the Scripture sence, the lawful Astrologian foretelling probable events, fore-seen by Natural causes upon any person, or Nation; as Deborah observed the Stars concerning Sicera and his Army (although she knew what should come to pass more certainly by the Spirit of Prophesie than by the Stars.) The unlawful Astrologian, or Planetarian foretelling things not only probably, but certain and necessarily to come to pass, as if there were such strong inclination, influence, and co-action in those Cælestial Bodies, as that our earthly bodies can no way avoyd them, and as if God hath no Decree but what may be fore-seen in the Stars. But the Scripture, and true Religion teacheth us otherwise, for as a man may not be so stupid as to deny the influence of the Stars, so no man may be so Atheistical as to deny that Divine Providence ruleth all inferiour bodies; not only in that sense, that Astra regunt homines and regit astra Deus, (which is the Astrologians Creed) but beyond the influence

of the Stars; otherwise it were in vain to pray to God for recovery from sickness, or loss, or calamity, because haply the Stars threaten death, or ruine; in vain it were then for the Elders of the Church to pray over the sick, with hope of their recovery, except the Stars say, Amen. In vain it were then for a Nation to fast, and pray for Peace when the Stars threaten War. In vain it were for a man to hope for prosperity in all his undertakings, by walking in Gods way (as is taught in Deut. 29.9.) because the Stars in that mans Nativity threaten evil, and no prosperity to the whole course of that mans life. But as a skilful Physitian may by good Phisical applications of remedies lengthen the days of a man, upon whom the Stars have a bad influence, and threaten death (which Astrologians themselves confess) how much more may true Religion in a man obtain a blessing for health, and prosperity, and peace, beyond what the Stars do promise? which is the whole discourse of Levit. chap. 26. therefore it must needs follow that Grace may turn away the bad influence, and Vice may hinder the good influence of the Stars from a Man, or a Nation; and they that were such meer Naturalists, as that under colour of their science in Astrologie they taught the people otherwise, they were seducing Witches; and they that did seek to such for Divinations, and did not regard Divine Providence to rule beyond the Stars influence, and so neglected seeking to God in time of trouble, they were Idolaters bewitched. Another way might Astrologians become Witches, that is, if an Astrologian finding that many of his Prognosticks happened true, and did thereby dissemble Prophesie, pretending that he did by Revelation, or prophetical Inspiration fore-tell those things which yet he did only conjecturally foresee by the Stars, that pretence or dissimulation made him a Witch, fit to seduce and mis-lead the people. So much for the Third description. The Fourth Description. THe Fourth description, or term of description; of a Witch in the text is Conjector, a Conjecturer; that was such a one that had some particular pretence or colour whereupon he grounded his Divinations, making the people beleeve that thereby he could Divine or Prophesie unto the people; whereas yet it was altogether a cousening imposture, or uncertain guessing, or conjecturing, and according to that he is here described by Moses as a Witch; what that Imposture was, Expositors have given several glosses, one Exposition is, That they observed the flying of Fowls, and thence gave their uncertain Predictions, or Divinations, but for that we finde no example in the Scriptures in the Original sence, and therefore leave it, and do also think, that to observe the flying of Fowls for Predictions of weather, as also the postures of Beasts, and creeping things is no offence, nor is here forbidden. Another exposition is, That they observed the intralls of Beasts, from whence they pretended they did know the will of the gods; and that was indeed of Beasts that were offered in Sacrifice to their Idols. By which pretence being but a meer cousening Imposture, they seduced the people to Idolatry, and therefore were reckoned and described among Witches in the text; and for that exposition we have that example in the Scriptures, Ezek. 21. 26. (which in Tremellius translation is thus) To use Divinations, he will furbush Knives, he will consult with Idols, he will look in the Liver, this is a plain demonstration of this Fourth description of a Witch in the text; that is, such a one as pretended to the people that their Idol gods hiding their secrets in the intralls of the sacrificed Beasts, he being one of their Priests, could by searching the intralls, conjecture to the people the meaning of the gods. This exposition is agreeable to that, 2 Chron. 33. 3. when Manasses had built Idol-Altars in the House of God, it followeth immediatly in the sixt verse, Et Divinationibus, and conjectationibus and prestigiis usus est; and he used Divinations, and Conjecturings, and Juglings, all tending to one end, to seduce the people to Idolatry, as followeth in the ninth verse, he made Judah and Jerusalem to go astray, for God had appointed his people not to inquire after uncertain conjecturings, by any Idol Impostures of the Heathen, but to inquire after himself, by the Prophets, and by his Priests, by an Ephod, by Urim and Thummim, as appeareth, I Sam. 30. 7. Exod. 28. 30. Some report that the Roman South-sayers did take the anckle bone of a Beast sacrificed, which bone was by them called talus in the Latine, the said bone is easie to be seen in the foot of any Oxe or Sheep, and hath four sides equally poysed, and being cast upon a Table it falleth contingently like a Dye; and therefore are the Dyes called by the same name in latin tali, and when those Idol Priests, the Roman South-sayers, would enquire of their Idols for Divinations, or rather give Divinations in the name of their Idols, they would cast that bone upon the Table, and according to the several contingent falling of the bone like the cast of a Dye, so they gave several conjecturing Divinations, every side when it chanced upward being of a several signification, given by their Idol, as they pretended; a meer cheating Imposture to seduce the people; a lively demonstration of it may be seen among Boys, casting the bone in the same manner in certain childish Games called cock-up-all. It may be collected also, That the Idol Priefts of the Heathen did sometimes use this imposture for one, (they having divers ways to delude the people) that was, for the Priest to be blinde-folded, and one or more to touch him, and he to conjecture or guess who it was that touched him; which was easily done by the confederacy of some stander by, some Priest like himself, who gave him a private token which the people did not take notice of, but were thereby deluded, and thought him to have a Prophetical inspiration from the Idol gods, and this is collected from Matth. 26. 68, especially if that place be compared with Mark 14. 65. where it appeareth, That the corrupt Jews, who had been defiled by the manner of the Heathen, did blind-fold Christ and smite him, and said, Prophefie, who it is that smote thee; they offering to try Christ by such ways as they had seen the Heathen try their Prophets by, who notwithstanding were Impostors and false Prophets. So much for the Fourth term, of description, of a Witch in the text, Conjector, a Conjecturer. The Fifth Description. The Fifth Appellation, or term of description of a Witch in the Text, is Prestigiator, that is, a Jugler. THe interpretation of this word is plain in the Scriptures, that is, one that worketh false or lying Wonders, or lying Miracles, in opposition of the true Miracles that were wrought by God, by his Prophets, such were Jannes, and Jambres, 2 Tim. 3. 8, 9. As Jannes and Jambres withstood Moses, soalso do these resist the truth; now how Jannes and Jambres withstood Moses it appeareth, Exod. 7.5. 8.9. God would have his Prophets, Moses, and Aaron to be known by their Miracles, that the people might beleeve that God had sent them, they wrought the Miracles that God had commanded them, Exod. 7. 13. but it appeareth in vers. 14. that these Juglers withstood them, and when the Messengers of God wrought true Miracles, those Witches wrought lying Miracles in opposition of them, Fecerunt similiter, they did the like. The Latin translation is thus; Tum vocavit Pharo sapientes and Prestigiatores, ut facerent ipsi quoq; magi Ægyptii suis incantationibus similiter; and Pharoah called the Wise men, and Juglers, that the Magicians of Ægypt might also do the like with their inchantments; so likewise vers. 25. Fecerunt similtier magis suis incantationibus, the Magicians did the like with their Inchantments; this word Similiter, the like, or in like manner, is of great importance, leaft some ignorant reader of the Scriptures should suppose, that the Magicians did the same Miracles that the Prophets did, whereas those acts of the Magicians were only delusions, (although enough to blind Pharaohs eyes, because God would harden his heart.) And as it appeareth in 2 Timi. 3. 9. their actions were only mad fooleries that came to light, and were proved ridiculous, as the words import, for the craft of Jugling, to them that are not acquainted with it, breedeth great admiration in the beholders, and seemeth, to filly people, to be miraculous, and yet being known is but deceit and foolery; so that the beholder himself cannot but blush, and be ashamed to think he was so easily cousened, and did so much admire a ridiculous Imposture, that craft of Jugling consisteth. First, In slight of hand, or cleanly conveyance. Secondly, In confederacy; and Thirdly, In the abuse of Natural Magick. The first is profitably seen in our common Juglers, that go up and down to play their Tricks in Fayrs and Markets, I will speak of one man more excelling in that craft than others, that went about in King James his time, and long since, who called himself, The Kings Majesties most excellent Hocus Pocus, and so was he called, because that at the playing of every Trick, he used to say, Hocus pocus, tontus talontus, vade celeriter jubeo, a dark composure of words, to blinde the eyes of the beholders, to make his Trick pass the more currantly without discovery, because when the eye and the ear of the beholder are both earnestly busied, the Trick is not so easily discovered, nor the Imposture discerned; the going about of this Fellow was very useful to the wise, to see how easily people among the ancient Heathen were deceived, in times and places of ignorance, for in these times many silly people (yea and some also that think themselves wise) will stand like Pharaoh and his Servants, and admire a Jugling Imposture; or like the silly Samaritans, Acts 8. 10. who did so much admire a seducing Jugler, as they said, He was the great power of God, until they saw the true and real Miracles of Philip, vers. 6. And others again on the contrary will stand affrighted, or run out of the room scared like fools, saying, The Devil is in the room, and helpeth him to do such Tricks; and some saying absolutely, He is a Witch, and ought to be hanged; when as he did only act the part of a Witch to enlighten, and not to deceive, that people might see and discern the Impostures by which the Idols of the Heathen were made famous, by their jugling Priests, and might laugh at their vanities (they that would see the manner of this part of Jugling, or cleanly conveyance more fully, may read Master Scots discovery of Witchcraft, where it is set down at large, to the satisfaction of all those that are not wilfully ignorant; as also briefly afterward in this Fifth description, after pag. 34. And now for illustrating of the History of Pharaobs Magicians, I will parallel this Hocus Pocus, or English Jugler, a little with them; they are called Prestigiatores, Juglers, Exod. 7. 14. and yet in the same verse, and also in vers. 25. it is said, they did in like manner by their inchantments; Why with their Inchantments? Not that Jugling and Inchanting are one and the same imposture, but the reason is, because when they wrought a Jugling Trick, or lying Miracle, they always spake a Charm, or Inchantation immediately before it, like to that of our English Jugler aforesaid, to make the delusion the stronger, by busying the senses of Hearing and Seeing in the Spectator both at once, for a Charm, or Inchantation was only a composure of words to delude people, who thought that words spoken in a strange manner had vertue and efficacy in them (as may be seen more fully in the Sixth description following) therefore are they said to work their false Miracles by their Inchantments, because they seemed to silly beholders to do them by their inchantations or words, when as indeed they did them only by slight of hand, or cleanly conveyance called Legerdemain; and they that are well acquainted with this craft of Jugling, may easily conceive how these Magicians did their Feats without so much admiring them, when they read the History, as if they had done great Wonders, which were only delusions; The second and third Miracle, that they

38

dissembled, do plainly appear in the letter of the History, Exod. 7. 2. they seemed to turn water into bloud, Fecerunt similiter, and yet mark well the History, and yee shall see there was no water in Ægypt, for Moses had turned it all into bloud before, vers. 20. 21. 24. 25. so then they could finde no River or Pond to do that feat in, it must needs follow then, that they sent for water where it was to be had, which was no nearer than Goshen, and so shewed a petty Jugling Trick before Pharaoh in a room, with a Bowl or Tray of water, setting it upon the ground, and by slight of hand conveying bloud into it to colour it; so likewise for the Third Miracle which they dissembled, Chap. 8. 7. it was necessarily done by a such vessel of water; for they could not finde any other water free in all Ægypt, which were nor already full of the abundance of Frogs, vers. 3. 5. and what common Jugler might not easily dissemble that Miracle, by setting a bowl of water down before Pharaoh and his Servants, and by slight of hand conveying in three or four Frogs, and so holding up their staffe, and speaking certain words to make it seem to silly spectators that the waters brought forth those Frogs; The first Miracle indeed seemeth more difficult to dissemble, and yet not so difficult if you saw it acted, for what is easier than for a cunning Jugler to hold up a staffe as if he would throw it down, and then to speak a lofty inchantation, to busie the intention of the Spectators, and then with slight of hand to throw down an artificial Serpent instead of his staffe, and convey away his staffe, that so they might think his staffe was turned into a Serpent, for these Histories are set down according to the apprehension of the deceived beholders, and not that the Magicians did them really, for then we must beleeve that they wrought real Miracles as the Prophets did, which were an ignorant and absurd tenent; whereas the Scriptures do manifest that they were only mad fooleries, and were discovered and came to light, 2 Tim. 3. 9. yet many are so stupid, that rather then they will not have them really done, they say they were really done by the power of the Devil, and so ascribe power to the Devil for working Miracles, whereas we never read in the Scriptures that the Devil may have any supernatural power ascribed to him, but is only the Father of Lyes. The same kinde of Jugling Tricks were the Impostures of Simon Magus, in Acts 8. 9. which although the people did for a time behold with admiration, yet when they saw real Miracles wrought by Philip, vers. 6. 12. they beleeved him, and not the Impostor any longer, for they did easily see a difference between real Miracles, and cheating Impostures. Some again will have it, that these Acts of Pharaohs Juglers, and others in the Scriptures might be real as they seemed to be, and yet brought to pass by the profoundness of the Art of Magick, which Art is of greater force (say they) than Jugling, or else why were they called in the same verse, Exod. 7. 11. Juglers, Wise men, and Magicians all at once? but let not any be so weak in understanding as to think, That any Art in the World could do that really that required a miraculous hand of power to do, for this is the essential or formal reason of a Miracle to be done by a power Supream, and beyond the power of Man or Devil, or the vertue of any Art; and for this word, Magicians, in its own proper sence it is taken for Wise and Learned men, in Astrologie, and other Arts wherein Schollers are instituted; and so there is no difference between [Greek omitted] and [Greek omitted] in the Greek, neither was it taken in any other sence among the ancient, and such were they that came to Christ and offered gifts, Matth. 2. 1. 11. called Magi; in this sence also it is said, That Moses was learned in all the wisdom of the Ægyptians, Acts 7. 22. and here in Exod. 7. 11. these Juglers are called Magi, Wise men, and Learned, because they pretend so, and were so thought by the people, whereas they were indeed but cheating Impostors, but because they and many other cousening Mates mentioned in the Scriptures, have by usurpation obtained that appellation from the people, Magicians, or Wise men, therefore it is used and taken by some Writers for such as use all cousening Diabolical Impostures; yet Moses here in this place of Exod. 7. 11. gave them not that manner of name or appellation, only Magicians, but withall describeth them by their peculier appellation, that is Juglers; and so in all the Old Testament, where Magician is taken in the worst sence, it is not set alone, but

40

conjoyned with some other terms of an Impostor for a more full description, so that a Magician in the worst sence in the Scripture phrase is only an Impostor, or Deceiver; in the best sence, a learned Wise man, therefore no real Miracle, but only delusions can bee wrought by Magick. I said a little before, That this craft of Jugling consisteth of three things; the First is, Slight of Hand, or cleanly conveyance; the Second is Confederacy, that is, when many or few agents do agree together in bringing to pass cheating impostures, contrary to the truth. An example of this wee have in the History of Bell, the Idol, in the Book of Daniel, which though it be called Apocripha, and doubtful whether it be a true History, yet this example whether it bee true or not, it doth plainly demonstrate the Witchcraft of Idol Priests by confederacy, which is one main arm of the craft of Jugling, Wisd. 14. 14. 20. it appeareth plain how they confederated together in extolling the Idol, to uphold it for their own delicious maintenance, and to seduce the King and people to Idolatry, by making them beleeve that Bell did eate up all the daily provision that was set before him, whereas they themselves, with their Wives and Children, came in at secret doors in the night, and did eate up and carry away all that was provided at the Kings charge, until Daniel discovered that their jugling imposture; and although there be not so plain a demonstration of the Jugling Impostures of every Idol spoken of in the Scriptures, yet no Idol but had the like delusions; for they built their Idol Houses on purpose with several slights, and secret conveyances to bring their Jugling Tricks to pass, and had daily new inventions of new Impostures whereby they deceived the World, and seduced them to Idolatry, therefore Elijah, I King. 18. 19. would not trust the Priests of Baal to remain in their own Idol House, when he would discover them to the people, but caused them all to come forth to Mount Carmel, and then he said, as in vers. 24. The God that answereth by fire, let him be God. Why did he cause the King to command them all to Mount Carmel? The reason was, because if they might have acted their part in their Idol House, being built with secret conveyances for all deceit, they might have secretly fired the

Oblation, and so might have deluded the people, still making them beleeve their Idol had answered them by fire, but being in Mount Carmel, remote from their Idol House, they could only act the part of Mad-men, cutting themselves that the people might have somewhat to gaze at, but could bring nothing to pass to save their credit, or their lives; the deluding impostures of the Priests of Baal, are called Præstigiæ Isabelæ 2 King. 9, 22 the Juglings or Witchcraft of Jezabel, because the being an Idolatrous Woman maintained those Priests of Baal in their Witchcraft, or delusions, to seduce the people to Idolatry. The third Branch whereupon this craft of Jugling consisteth, is the abuse of Natural Magick, that is, the abuse of their knowledge in Natural causes, as for instance in some few; take Woolfs dung, and carry it in your pocket that it may take the heat of your body, and it will make any mad Bull, or other Cattel of that kinde to fly from you, and to run very farre away from their pasture to the admiration of the beholders. Take a peece of paper and rub one part of it with fresh Lemmon peele, and dry it again a little, and then dip your Pen in Inke, that is made of stone blew, steeped two or three days in cold water, and write upon the place that had the tincture of the Lemmon peele, and it will write a pure bright red, and then with the same Pen and Inke write upon another place of the paper, and it writeth blew, whereby there is caused great admiration in the beholders, to see a man with one Pen, and one and the same Inke write red and blew. Albartus Magnus, and also Misaldus do write of many wonderful things that may be done by the knowledge of Natural causes, or the secrets of Nature, which although many of them be false, yet for such as are true, they may bee lawfully done; and therein we may glorifie God, in beholding the wonderful Works of his hands, in the secret causes of things. But now for the abuse of these things, as namely by the doing of these things to seduce the people, by making silly people beleeve we do them by a miraculous power, thereby pretending our selves to be Prophets, as did Simon Magus in the Acts; this is right Jugling Witchcraft, or to make the people beleeve that they are done by the power of some Idol, thereby to seduce the people, or any way to affront the Prophets, by comparing them with true Miracles, to withstand the truth, as Pharaohs Magicians did, were right Witchcraft. So likewise for the Oyntment called Unguentum armarium, or Weapon salve (that is an Oyntment made of such ingredients, as by anointing the Weapon wherewith a man or beast is wounded, it healeth the Wound (if it be true by certain experience, as many Phisitians and Chyrurgions do affirm) it may lawfully be used, and we may glorifie God in the use of it, who hath given such excellent secret qualities to the Creatures, which are made for the use of man. Also Jacob used the peeled rods, which by their secret operation being set before the sheep in the heat of their Generation, caused them, by beholding them in their conceiving, to conceive and bring forth party coloured Lambs; but if any man shall use these secrets to this end to make the people beleeve they are Prophets, and do them by a miraculous power, that so they may seduce the people to errour under a colour of working Miracles, such men are seducing Witches. Thus a Planetarian abusing the lawful Science of Astrologie may become a Witch, not only under the notion of a Planetarian, but of a Jugler; as for instance, Pedro Mexia, a Spanish Historian, writeth of one Columbus, who coming to an Island in the new-found World called Hispaniola, desired Traffick with the Natives for Victuals, which they denying, he told them they should all dye of the Plague, and for a sign hereof they should see the Moon as red as bloud at such a time, and contrary to her former condition; afterward they beholding the Moon eclipsed at the same time fore-told by Columbus, and knowing no rules of Astrologie, they beleeved his words and craved pardon, and brought him supply of Victuals; This was but a remiss degree of deceiving Witch-craft, or rather a Cheat, because it tended not to Idolatry, but yet in the act it self, pretending falsly a miraculous power, it was Jugling Witch-craft. It is now fully demonstrated what a Jugler is in the Scripture sence, but yet Moses mentioneth both Sexes in the Scriptures, for it is written, Exod. 22. 18. Præstigiatricem ne sinito vivere, suffer not a Jugling Woman to live. This is not any thing different in Nature from Præstigiator a Jugling man, but only in Sex, as if he had said, As you ought not to suffer Jugling seducing men to live, so likewise if there be a Woman found among you that useth this craft of working false Miracles, to delude and seduce the people to Idolatry, although she be the weaker Sex, to whom mercy might seem to be due, yet suffer her not to live; all one in sence with that Levit. 20. 27 where Witches of both Sexes are mentioned in one verse; If a man or woman be a giver of Oracles, or Divinations, or a South-sayer, they shall be put to death; yet whereas Moses, in all the Law, speaketh more fully of Witches in the Masculine, than in the female Sex; it confuteth that common tradition of people that Witches are most of the female Sex. Here I am compelled (for the satisfaction of some that are so weak in capacity that they will rather stand to cavil in a disputative way, than to understand things that are not in themselves disputative, but demonstrative) to demonstrate some few of the most admired Tricks of common Jugling. First, A Jugler knowing the common tradition, and foolish opinion that a familiar Spirit in some bodily shape must be had for the doing of strange things, beyond the Vulgar capacity, he therefore carrieth about him the skin of a Mouse stopped with feathers, or some like Artificial thing, and in the hinder part there of sticketh a small springing Wire of about a foot long, or longer, and when he begins to aet his part in a Fayr, or a Market before Vulgar people, he bringeth forth his Impe, and maketh it spring from him once or twice upon the Table, and then catcheth it up, saying, would you be gone? I will make you stay and play some Tricks for me before you go, and then he nimbly sticketh one end of the Wire upon his waste, and maketh his Impe spring up three or four times to his shoulder, and nimbly catcheth it, and pulleth it down again every time, saying, Would you be gone? in troth if you be gone I can play no Tricks, or Feats of Activity to day, and then holdeth it fast in one hand, and beateth it with the other, and slily maketh a squeeking noyse with his lips, as if his Impe cried, and then putteth his Impe in his breeches, or in his pocket, saying, I will make you stay, would you be gone? Then begin the silly people to wonder, and whisper, then he sheweth many slights of activity as if he did them by the help of his Familiar, which the silliest sort of beholders do verily beleeve; amongst which he espyeth one or other young Boy or Wench, and layeth a tester or shilling in his hand wetted, and biddeth him hold it fast, but whilst the said Boy, or silly Wench thinketh to enclose the peece of silver fast in the hand, he nimbly taketh it away with his finger, and hasteneth the holder of it to close his hand, saying, Hold fast or it will be gone, and then mumbleth certain words, and crieth by the vertue of Hocus, Pocus, hay passe prestor, be gone; now open your hand, and the silly Boy or Wench, and the beholders stand amazed to see that there is nothing left in the hand; and then for the confirmation of the wonder, a Confederate with the Jugler, standeth up among the crowd (in habit like some country-man or stranget that came in like the rest of the people) saying, I will lay with you forty shillings you shall not convey a shilling out of my hand; it is done saith the Jugler, take you this shilling in your hand, yea marry (saith he) and I will hold it so fast as if you get it from me by words speaking, I will say you speak in the Devils name, and with that he looketh in his hand in the sight of all the people, saying, I am sure I have it, and then claspeth his hand very close, and layeth his other hand to it also, pretending to hold it the faster, but withall slily conveyeth away the shilling into his glove, or into his pocket, and then the Jugler cryeth, Hay passe, presto vade, jubco, by the vertue of Hocus Pocus, tis gone, then the Confederate openeth his hand, and in a dissembling manner saineth himself much to wonder, that all that are present may likewife wonder, then the Jugler calleth to his Boy, and biddeth him bring him a glass of Claret Wine, which hee taketh in his hand and drinketh, and the he taketh out of his bagge a tonnel made of Tin, or Latine double, in which double device he hath formerly put so much claret wine as will almost fill the glass again, and stopping this tonnel at the little end with his finger, turneth it up that all may behold it to be empty, and then setteth it to his fore-head, and taketh away his finger, and letteth the Wine run into the Glass, the filly Spectators thinking it to be the fame wine which he drank to come again out of his fore-head;

then he faith, If this be not enough I will draw good Claret Wine out of a post, and then taketh out of his bagge a Wine-gimblet, and so he pierceth the Post quite thorow with his Gimblet; and then is one of his boys on the other sfide of the wall with a Bladder and a Pipe (like as when a Clister is administred by the Phisician) and conveyeth the Wine to his Master thorow the Post, which his Master (Vintner like) draweth forth into a Pot, and filleth it into a Glass, and giveth the company to drink. Another way it is very craftily done by a Spanish Borachio, that is a Leather Bottle as thin and little as a Glove, the neck whereof is about a foot long, with a screw at the top instead of a stopple; this Bottle the Jugler holdeth under his arm, and letteth the neck of it come along to his hand under the sleeve of his Coat, and with the fame hand taketh the tax in the fasset that is in the post, and yet holdeth the tax half in and half out, and crusheth the Bottle with his arm, and with his other hand holdeth a Wine-pot to the tax, so that it seemeth to the beholders that the Wine cometh out of the tax, which yet cometh out of the Bottle, and then he giveth it among the company to drink; and being all drunk up but one small glass at the last, he calleth to his Boy, saying, Come sirrah, you would faine have a cup, but his Boy makeeth answer in a disdainful manner, saying, No Master not I, if that be good Wine that is drawn out of a Post I will lose my head; yea sirrah saith his Master, then your head you shall lose; come sirrah, you shall go to pot for that word; then he layeth his Boy down upon the Table upon a Carpet, with his face downward, commanding him to lye still, then he taketh a linnen cloth, and spreadeth it upon the Boys head broad upon the table, and by slight of hand conveyeth under the cloth a Head with a face, limned so like his Boys Head and Face that it is not discerned from it; then hee draweth forth his Sword or Falchion, and seemeth to cut off his Boys head; but withall it is to be noted, That the confederating Boy putteth his head thorow a slit in the Carper, and thorow a hole in the Table made on purpose, yet unknown to the Spectators, and his Master also by slight of hand layeth to the Boys shoulder a peece of wood made concave at one end like a scuppit, and round at the other end like a mans neck with the head cut off, the concave end is hidden under the Boys shirt, and the other end appeareth to the company very dismal (being limbned over by the cunning Limbner) like a bloudy neck, so lively in shew that the very bone and marrow of the neck appeareth, insomuch that some Spectators have fainted at the sight hereof; then he taketh up the false Head aforesaid by the hair, and layeth it in a Charger at the feet of the Boy, leaving the bare bloudy neck to the view of the deluded beholders, some gazing upon the neck, some upon the head, which looketh gashful, some beholding the Corps tremble like a body new slain; then he walketh by the Table, faying to the head, and the seeming dead Corps, Ah ha, sirrah, you would rather lose your Head then drink your Drink, but preseutly he smiteth his hand upon his breast, saying, To speak the very truth in cool bloud, the fault did not deserve death, therefore I had best set on his Head again; then he spreadeth his broad linnen cloth upon the Head and taketh it out of the Charger, and layeth it to the shoulders of the Corps, and by slight of hand conveyeth both the Head and the false neck into his Bagge, and the Boy raiseth up his Head from under the Table; then his Master taketh away the linnen cloth that was spread upon him, and saith, By the vertue of Hocus pocus, and Fortumatus his Night-cap, I wish thou mayest live again; then the Boy riseth up safe and well, to the admiration of the deluded beholders. These and the like Jugling Tricks (some whereof are done meerly by slight of hand, some have a help from false Instruments, as false Knives, false Boxes, false Locks, false Wasecoats, and the like, are many of them demonstrated by Master Scot, and many are daily invented, which are all done by common reason, without the least compact with the Devil, (unless they do them to feduce, and then the Devil is indeed in their heart, as he was in Simon Magus, in the Acts, and is in every wicked man.) And yet sometimes it hapneth, that if here have been any University Schollars at the beholding, or at the acting of these common Tricks, they have gone out and fallen into a dispute upon the matter, some saying, Sensus nunquam fallitur circa proprium objectum, some have said that the Jugler by his Familiar doth thicken the Air, some again that he hurteth the Eye-sight, and so deceiveth the beholders; and in all their discourse they shew themselves very Philosophical, but very little capacious. And Cosper writing upon that subject, hath pretended to shew himself Theological, but betrayeth himself to be very silly, blinde, and ignorant. It being fully demonstrated what a Jugler is in the Scripture sence, let every one consider seriously who be the Juglers, of this and former Ages, that ought to be put to death by the Law of Moses, we might think that no man were so silly and foolish to think that it is meant common Juglers, who play their Tricks in Fayers and Markets, nor Gentlemen who sometimes in imitation of them, do in sport, play Tricks of slight of hand, or legerdemain, with confederates or without, for it is most certain and true, that if it bee rightly understood, that these do a great deal of good, that recreation tending rightly to the illumination of people of all sorts, to shew them the vanity and ridiculousness of those delusions and lying Wonders, by which men were so easily deluded in old times by Pharaohs Magicians, by Simon Magus, and Elimas the Sorcerer, and now adays by our professed Wizzards, or Witches, commonly called Cunning Men, or good Witches, who will undertake to shew the face of the Thief in the Glass, or of any other that hath done his Neighbour wrong privily, when as they do all by Jugling delusions, and are themselves right Witches, that cause men to seek to the Devil for help, that will undertake and promise to unwitch people that are (as sools commonly say) bewitched; these common sporting Juglers also may illuminate people to see the Jugling Witchcraft of Popish Priests, in causing Rhoods to move their eyes and hands in compassion to peoples prayers, of which you may read more fully afterward. Yet in Queen Elizabeths time, as appeareth in Mr. Scots Discovery of Witchcraft, in the fifteenth Book, Chap. 42. there was a Master of Arts condemned only for using himself to the study and practise of the Jugling craft, how justly I will not controvert; but this I say, That if a man may not study and practise the discovery of Cheats without being a Cheater, nor the discovery of Witchcraft without being accounted a Witch, it is the way for Witches and Cheaters to play their pranks, and no man able to tax them, or accuse them, or to say who they are that are Witches; and this foolish nice censuring, and ignorant condemning hath bred great and general ignorance of this subject of Witchcraft; which God himself describeth so often in the Scriptures, for people to know and avoyd the practise of seducing, or being seduced by it, but for that Master of Arts before named, the Lord of Leicester having more wisdom in some things than some had, did protect him for a time after he was condemned, but what became of him is not mentioned, but yet if he had been a Jugler, or practiser of that Craft to this end, to withstand the Prophets when they wrought true Miracles, as Pharaohs Juglers withstood Moses, or if he were one that practised it to seduce the people after lying delusions, to magnifie himself as a false Prophet, like Simon Magus in the Acts, or to cause people to ascribe miraculous power to him, or to seek to the Devil as our common Deceivers, called good Witches, do, he was deservedly condemned; but to study Witchcraft, and actually to demonstrate it by practise, to shew how easily people were and may be deluded by it (seeing God hath commanded Witches to be put to death, and what they were or are, is not now adays fully understood (no not by the Learned) is no more deserving death than for Master Scot to write a book in the discovery of it, or for a Minister to discover to the people the danger of an Idol; to which Witchcraft is necessarily joyned as an upholder and companion, or for a Minister to shew the secret and dangerous mature, and several windings of Sin and Satan; for the essence of a Witch is not in doing false Miracles, or any other Witchcraft by demonstration or discovery, but in seducing people from God, and his Truth; As for example, Pharaohs Magicians in that they did throw down their staffe, and made it seeme to be turned into a Serpent, to the end to withstand Moses, and to seduce the Ægyptians, they were absolute Witches, but if any man now do the very same, or had then done it to discover the Jugling deceit of it, hee is no Witch, but a teacher and instructer of the people. So again for another example, he that goeth behinde a Rhood, or other Popish Image, and draweth the secret Wiers that causeth the eyes and hands of the Image to move, to the end to delude and seduce the people to Idolatry, by admiration of it, as Popish Priests do; he is an absolute Witch, but he that goes behind it, and acteth the same part, and then cometh out and sheweth people the Imposture, and sheweth them the Wyers and secret delusious, is not a Witch, but a discoverer of a Witch (that did it to the end to seduce) and a Teacher and illuminator of the people. See more in the Sixth description. But we must know that in Queen Elizabeths time the Protestant Religion being then in its minority, when as Popery was but only suppressed, and not worn out of the memory, nor out of the hearts and affections of men (that yet in outward shew were Protestants) it was a brief tenent in the Universities, that he that did but study and contemplate upon this subject of Witchcraft was a dealer with unlawful and vain Science, and ought to be censured for a Witch, and by this subtill tradition they feared all Students, that no man dared to search into the bowels and secrets of that Craft, least (as they knew full well) thereby he should discover to the World the secret Impostures of the Popish Religion, which is altogether upheld by Witchcraft, of which Religion, many stood daily in expectation to have it set on foot as bries as ever, when (as they hoped) the times would change. Hath God given nine several descriptions of Witchcraft at once? Deut. 18. 10, 11. and reiterated them in many places of Scripture that we might take notice, who and what they are, with the Mystery of iniquity, and delusions that they practised? and shall not we study and contemplate upon it? by this vain tradition were many of their devillish Witchcrafts concealed, and came not to light, for many years, to the view or the world; example of that Popish Idol, Cheapside Crosse, which stood for many years like the Golden Image of Nebuchadnezzar, few men knowing the jugling Witchcraft that was therein, untill at the command of the Parliament it being pulled down, there were found therein the severall slights to move the Arms, Eyes, and Heads of the Images, and the Pipes to convey the water to make the Images shed tears in compassion to the peoples prayers, and to convey Milk into the breasts of the Image of the Virgin Mary, that the poor deluded people (seeing such lying Wonders, as Images of Gold, to move, to weep, and shed tears in abundance, and Milk to drop out of the Virgins breasts, through her earnest labouring with her Sontohear, and grant the prayers of the people) went home, bewitched to that devillish Idolatry by that grand Witch, that Whore of Rome that hath deceived all Nations with her Witchcraft, Revel. 18. 23. yet, to the grief of the hearts of this Popish crew, in the beginning of the reign of Queen Elizabeth, many of their devillish Witchcrafts were daily discovered, as in Master Lamberts Book of the Perambulation of Kent it appeareth, was discovered the Rhood of grace in Kent, who was always accompanied and helped by little St. Rumball, which Idol as Mr. Scot noteth in Lib.7.Chap. 6. was not inferiour in all deluding Impostures to the great Idol Apollo (or Apollos Oracle) whose Priests were the grand Witches of the World in its time) yet afterward the wires that made the eyes of the Images to goggle, and the Pins and Instruments for several delusions were discovered, with all the Witchcraft of the jugling Priests, with every circumstance thereof, which Image and Instruments were openly burnt together, by the authority and command of the Queen. And now it falleth in my way to speak of another grand Witch of the World, that is, Mahomet, the great Idol of the Turks, who by his Juglings and Divinations hath seduced a great part of the World to an Idolatrous worship, so absurd and silly, that his Disciples are ashamed to let any Christians come neer the place of his supposed Sepulchre at Mecha, lest they should laugh at their folly in worshipping an Iron Sepulchre, therefore all Christians are forbidden to come within five miles of that place upon pain of death; and because various reports have been abroad by several Authors concerning this Deceiver of the world, I will only cite the most allowable reports confirmed by Lampadius in Mellificio Historico, and also by Gulielmus Biddulphus an English Travellor (called, The Travels of certain English-men into farre Countries) very agreeable to the foresaid Lampadius;)

This devillish Impostor Mahomet desiring to magnifie himself among the people, did first of all delude his Wife, making her beleeve that he was a Prophet of God, for having the Falling-sickness, with which he fell often, and lay like a man in a trance, he told his Wife that Gabriel the Arch-angel did often appear to him, and reveal secrets from Heaven, and for the confirmation there of Sergius a wicked Monck, who was his instructer, affirmed, That Gnbriel did use to appear to all Prophets, and so both of them together did perswade the silly Woman that the reason of his falling in a Trance was, because the Angel was so glorious that he was not able to behold him without falling, and that all the time of his lying thus prostrate the Angel was talking with him; this silly Woman rejoycing in this; That she was married to a Prophet, reported the thing among other Women, so that in time this fellow obtained among pratling Women, and common people, the name of a Prophet; the Devil by this fellow taking occasion, and waiting his opportunity to deceive the World (as also by Sergius the Monck who was his companion) it hapned about the year of our Lord Christ, 591. about which time also began the Antichristian Popedome at Rome) that Heraclius the Roman Emperour, makeing use of the Armies of the Sarazens against the Persians, (and not giving them their daily pay, or stipend, which they expected and required of his Captains over them) they revolted from him; then this Mahomet, with his companion Sergius seconding him) became the Head of the Rebellion, or at least desired so to be thought by the people, that so he might any way become great among them; but the Souldiers not much regarding him, Sergius and he did so use their wits to perswade them, telling them, That he was ordained by God to that end, and sent by the Angel Gabriel to bring the people to the worship of God by the power of the Sword (for said he, Christ came only by Miracles and Signs to perswade, but I am the next Prophet, and the last that shall come, and am to compel people by the Sword) so that partly by subtilty, and partly by compulsion hee drew a mighty Army to him, to the overthrow of the Emperours power in those parts, from whence came that mighty Empire of the Turks; and because that Sergius had counselled him, that the only way to increase in strength was to set up a New Religion, he gathered unto him besides Sergius, John Presbyter an Arrian Heretick, and Selan a Jewish Astrologian, and another Barran, Persam Jacobitam; who together, that they might draw all people after him, Coyned a Religion, partly of the Circumcision, that so he might win the Jews, and the Saracens (who coming of Ishmael, do use the Circumcision of Abraham to this day) and were called Saracens, because Hagar was Sarahs Maid, and Hagarens from their Mother Hagar) and partly of Christianity, that so he might win Christians (for the Turks do acknowledge Christ to have been a Prophet, but they deny his Divinity, and his satisfaction for the Sins of Man, for they say that God had no Wife, and therefore could have no Son; and of this and the like silly conceits is composed the Turkish Alcoran) and that he might distinguish his Sect from Jews and Christians, he hath instituted his Sabbath on the Friday, and for the inticing of all men to his Religion, he telleth them, That they that fight boldly for his Worship, shall (if they bee slain) enter directly into Paradice, where they shall injoy plenty of pleasures, meat, and drink, and pretty Wenches abundance, and with these hopes (saith Lampadius) his Souldiers are so bewitched that they are always furious and greedy of fighting, be their danger never so great. Much more is reported of this Impostor by several Historians, but I have only described him briefly by these his seducements, (although he had many more) wherein may be noted that he was a Jugling false Prophet, in faining himself to be in extafie of minde, in a miraculous manner talking with the Angel Gabriel (according to this fifth term of description in the text) whereas he was only visited with the fits of his Epileptick disease; and in that he pretended these absurd Fantafies to be revealed to him by the Angel, he was a Diviner, and a lying Enthusiast (according to the second term of description in the text) in both which sense Sergius the Monck, and the rest of his Companions aforesaid, who joyned with him in his delusions, were Witches also; and herein it is strange to see the world of people that are infatuated by so groundless a Religion, for were it not for the stupidity of mens mindes and understanding, God did enough discover this Mahomet (the founder of this Turkish Religion) to bee an Impostor) at his death, for when hee boasted himself that at his death he would rise again the third day as Christ did, Albunar, one of his Disciples, to try the truth of his Doctrins and vaticiniations, gave him a cup of deadly poyson, which being drunk he swelled and dyed, and some hoping to see his Resurrection let him lye twelve days above ground, untill he stunk so intollerably that all men left him; and upon the twelfth day Albunar coming to view his Corps found his bones almost bare, his flesh being eaten with Doggs; wherefore he gathered his bones together and buried them in a pot, yet for the establishing of the Empire, to his Succesfors, they maintain still-his Religion, and have made him an Iron Sepulchre at Mecha. So much for the Fifth description of a Witch in the text, Prestigiator, a Jugler.

The Sixth Description. THe Sixth description of a Witch in the Text, is, Incantater, or Utens incantatione, that is, an Inchanter, or user of Charms, or a Charmer. A Charm (as is said before in the Fifth description) is only a strange composure of words to blinde the understandings of people, it pretending that by vertue of words great matters were brought to pass, and these Charms were used either before a Jugling Trick, to busie the mindes of the Spectators, to make the Trick pass the more currently without being perceived, as Pharaohs Juglers used them, who are said to do that which they did with their Inchantments, because they seemed to do things by vertue of words spoken, which were not done at all, but only dissembled by the jugling craft; (which demonstration of a Charm, or Incantation used in that kinde is also set down in the Fifth description) or else otherwise these Charms were used or spoken alone without a Jugling slight, and thereby was pretended, that by vertue of such and such words spoken, such things should come to pass as the party desired, who inquired after Charmers for matters of concernment; sometimes these Charms were given in writing for a man to wear about his neck, or to carry in his pocket, pretending that by vertue of those words his matters should be brought to pass, whereas words of themselves either spoken, or written, have no force to bring any thing to pass; neither was it the word Ephatha, Mark 7. 34. that opened the ears of the deaf (as some inchanting Wizards would make people beleeve it was) but the power of him that spake it; yet such was the manner of the Idol Priests, and false Prophets, that whereas Gods Prophets spake words in the name of the Lord, and the things they spake came to pass by Gods power, those Idol Priests and false Prophets pretended, that by vertue of words they could bring to pass the like, and so they led the people a whoring after them, to regard more their foolish deluding Charms, than the power of God, that bringeth all things to pass.

The Roman South-sayers gave their Charms in verse, from whence is derived the word Charns, from Carmex, signifying a Verse, or a Charm; the manner of Charms sometimes consisted in blessing and cursing, the Inchanter pretending, That by vertue of a Charm he could bless, and that they were blessed that carried such words about them written in a paper, or that had such words spoken to them, or in their behalf by the Charms; and that by vertue of an Incantation pronounced against any man, that man was cursed, and that he that carried such a Charm with him, his enemies were cursed, and should fall before him. Elisha indeed cursed two and forty Children in the name of the Lord, and they were accursed, because it was the wrath of God pronounced against them by his Prophet, 2 King. 2. 23. but hee that imputeth it to the vertue of a Curse, and useth such words as Elisha spake to bring such a thing to pass, against an enemy, without warrant from God, hee is an inchanting Witch; and he that trusteth to such words meerly for the vertue of words, either of blessing or cursing, is an Idolater, not discerning the power of God, the Curse without cause shall not come, Prov. 3. 33. neither shall blessing or cursing prevail any thing if it be not from the Lord; if Micaiah had Prophesied good to the King of Israel, as he would have had him, it had not availed, but it had been a meer Charm, that is, a meer composure of unwarranted words, I King. 22. 13.

and yet his false Prophets could please him well, making him beleeve that by vertue of their pretended Prophesie (which was but a meer Charm) all things should go well with him, I King. 22. 10, 11, 12. A more plain demonstration of this Discourse is the History of Balaam, Numb. 22. 6. Balac sent to Balaam to Curse the people of Israel, but he concludeth, Numb. 23. 27. there is no inchanting against Israel, for had Balaam played the inchanting Witch, as Balac would have had him, it had availed nothing, because Charms are of no force, no more than Divinations, which are only given by deceiving Witches to cheat Idolatrous fools of their mony. And in Chap. 24. vers. I. it is said, Balaam went not as formerly to fetch Inchantments, or Incantations, that is, groundless and unwarranted Execrations, which are but Charms of no force, but only to delude the Hearers; for it is understood in the Chapter and Verse aforesaid, not that Balaam had formerly gone to fetch Incantations, for it is said in Chap. 22. vers. 19. and chap. 23. 3, 4, 5. verses, he went to inquire of the Lord; but here in Chap. 24. I. it is spoken according to the intention of Balak and his Princes, for they desired that Balaam would but curse Israel, whether he had warrant or not, supposing the words being but spoken by him were sufficient, as is said in Chap. 22. vers. 6. and Chap 23. vers. 11. which intention of theirs is here in Chap. 24. vers. I. called fetching of Incantations, for it implyeth the foolish supposition of Balak and his Princes, which they expressed in chap. 22. vers. 6. That whomsoever Balaam cursed were accursed, and whom he blessed were blessed; for if a very Prophet should so farre transgress, and go without warrant from God in blessing and cursing, or Prophecying, that Prophet were no more a Prophet, but an inchanting deluding Witch, and his words would not be worth regarding; and this is a sufficient demonstration of a Charmer, or Inchanter, or user of Incantations, being the Sixth term of description in the text, that is, that maketh any composure of words to delude the people, pretending to the people any vertue in words to bring things to pass, and so causeth people not to discern the power of God that bringeth all things to pass, but to impute things to the power of words, being but Charms, or Incantations. And indeed the fore-named History of Balaam, if it be rightly observed, is a large and a plain demonstration of the vanity of this sort of Witchcraft, whereby people were commonly seduced by false Prophets, or Witches, by listening only to the sound of words, and not to God the only disposer and bringer of all things to pass; for it appeareth in the History, that when Balak had caused Balaam to try all the ways that could be to curse the people by Charms, and he could not (because God gave him no warrant, and he knew it was in vain to do it without warrant) yet Balaam transgressing the word and command of God, shewed to Balak the only way to bring a Curse upon Israel indeed, and that was by seducing them to Idolatry, and causing their God to bee angry with them, as appeareth, Numb. 24. 14. where it is to be marked, That although in that verse this counsel of Balaam to Balak is not set down at large, yet the effect thereof appeareth in the next Chapter, and also in Revel. 2. 14. and Jude, vers. 11. where we may see that Balaam for reward taught Balak to lay a stumbling-block before the people, to cause them to fall, that stumbling-block were the Idols of Moab, which they being defiled withall, brought down the frowns of God upon them, Numb. 25. 3. but to hurt them with Charms or Incantations, was a vain and Idolatrous superftition of Balak, and if Balaam had answered his expectation, he had been indeed a Jugling Witch. The manner of Heathen Kings was, to strengthen themselves in their Kingdom (as they thought in their Idolatrous credulity) by these Inchantments, supposing, that if their inchanting false Prophets, (which were also Planetarians, and South-sayers, and Jugling deluders) did but utter their Inchantments, (being pretended Prophecies, and cursings artificially composed) against their enemies, that then their enemies should fall before them; and this is manifest in the Scriptures, not only of Balak, but of the King of Babel, and of the Chaldeans, Isa.47.12. Stand now with they Inchantments wherewith thou haft laboured from thy youth, if perhaps thou maist profit, if perhaps thou shalt shew thy self strong. This also was Ahabs Idolatry, when he desired Micaiah to Prophesie good unto him against Ramoth Gilead, thinking by vertue of ungrounded Prophecie (which had been but a meer composed Charm) hee should prevail, I King. 22. 13. Here may arise a Question, Whether every one that curseth his Neighbour be a Witch or not, according to this Sixth description in the text? To this I answer, That all blessing and cursing is not the formal essence of an Inchanter, for every one ought to bless, Luke, 6, 28. and he indeed that curseth his Neighbour, saying, A Plague take him, or I would be might break his neck, or never come home again, is a cursing railer, like Shimei, and a wicked breaker of Gods Law, for we ought to pray for our enemies; but all this kinde of passionate cursing doth not make an Inchanter, or Witch, but that blessing or cursing that maketh an Inchanter or Witch, or is of the essence of an Inchanter, is the professed craft of composing blessings and cursings, whereby they drew the people a whoring after them, making them beleeve, that by vertue of Charms, whomsoever they blessed were blessed, and whom they cursed were accursed, as Balak and his Princes being trained up in that kinde of Idolatry, thought, and said of Balaam; and had Balaam answered them according to their expectations, he had been an Inchanter, or Witch, or false Prophet; this description of a Charmer, as also all the nine terms of description of a Witch in the text, being only descriptions of false Prophets that seduced the people; and whereas Gods Prophets blessed in the name of the Lord, as Isaac blessed Jacob, or cursed, or pronounced a Curse, as Elisha against the forty and two Children, 2 King. 2. 24. and in all this, and in all other Prophesyings they did nothing of themselves, nor could any whit transgress the Word of the Lord; so on the contrary, false Prophets would give Divinations for rewards without any warrant or command from God; as Balak supposing Balaam would doe, sent the reward of Divinations, Numb. 22. 7. (that is there to be taken) he sent the reward of Inchantments, or Incantations; for Divinations against any man, that is unwarranted Prophesying against any man, is Inchantments (Divinations properly pretending Predictions, and manifestation of things hidden, being the Second description) but to use any composure of Divining words, thereby to cause any thing to come to pass, as Balak thought Balaam could do, and as Ahab thought Micaiah could doe, is Incantation, or Inchanting here. Here may arise another Question, Whether was Balaam a Witch or not, as some have supposed? Answ. If he was a Witch, it must be according to some one term of description in Deut. 18. 10, 11, but which of these can we call him? Inchanter he was none, for he refused to do it, although he was offered a reward. Surely Balaam was a Prophet of God, whom Balak thought could bring things to pass by his own power, he not discerning the power of God. All that we read of him in uttering of his Parables was to this end, That Israel was blessed, and Incantations or Cursing could not hurt them. 2 The History is a real Prophecie acted, by Balaam by Gods appointment, concluding all in this one Doctrin, That the only way to bewitch Israel, was, to lay stumbling-blocks before them, to insnare them with sins, and to bring down Gods Judgements upon them, Numb: 24. 14. Revel. 2. 14. yet the calling of this a Prophecie seemeth to be contradictory to the Scriptures, for how could he be said to be a Prophet of God, that taught Balak how to bring a curse upon Israel? but if we mark well the History, it may seem to some to be ful of contradictions, as in Numb. 22. 12. God said to Balaam, Go not, and vers. 20. Rise up and go with them; and vers. 22. The wrath of God was kindled because he went; and vers. 34. Balaam said, If it displease thee, I will return home again; and vers. 35. The Angel said, Go with the men; what is the meaning of this, go not, and yet go so often repeated? That is, go not according to the hire and request of Balak to play the Inchanter, but go to do the work of a Prophet, to shew the vanity of Balak his thoughts, who thinketh that words can prevail either to Bless or to Curse without warrant from God; and so Balaam as a Prophet obeyed the Lord, and did as the Lord commanded him, as appeareth in all the History; but yet it appeareth, Revel. 2, 14. hee taught Balak to lay a stumbling-block before the people, was that the part of a Prophet? yea according to the fore-named seeming contradictions it was, and it was not; for in the truth of the Doctrin that he delivered to Balak, that that was the only way to bring a Curse upon the people, to cause them to commit Idolatry, it was the part of a Prophet, but in that it became a snare to Israel, it was the part of a Witch, or a false Prophet, yet God would have such a thing come to pass by his Prophet for the full illustration of this Doctrin in the Scriptures, (for our sakes) that no Inchantment can hust us, but the only thing that can hurt any man is sinning against God, as God hath taught us elsewhere, Deut. 28. the fourteen first verses, the only way to be blest, is, to keep the Commandements of God, and from vers. 15. to the end of the Chapter, the only way to be accurst, is, to disobey God, and break his Commandements, And whereas Balaam was blamed, and afterward slain for teaching this Doctrin so plain to Balak, who abused it to insnare Israel, yet God hath taught us the same Doctrin, that we might know with Israel, and by Israels example, that nothing can hurt us but sin. So we may conclude of Balaam, that he was a Prophet, and yet acted the part of a Prophet and a Witch both at once (at least) a Prophet, in that his Doctrine was true, a Witch, in that hee taught Balak to play the Witch, that is, to draw the people to Idolatry, according to the First description, which is the very essence of Witchcraft; and although God would have this thing come to pass for our instruction, yet this was the errour of Balaam, That hee had laid open to Balak the way to bewitch the people, and in this only he transgressed, he did that which God had not commanded him, as some other Prophets did besides him, I King. 13. 18, 19, 22. To this Sixth description of a Witch in the text, is referred that place in Jerem. 23. 10. so commonly falsly interpreted as falsly translated, Because of Oathes the Land mourneth, as if it were meant of common Swearing, which although Swearing be a wicked thing, yet what room is there in that place for Swearing? unless yee will bring it in abruptly by head and shoulders, what coherence is there? Tremelius ttanslateth it thus, The Land is full of Adulterers, and because of Execrations the Land mourneth; Execrations is there taken for Incantations, being by a Synechdoche put for all kind of

Witchcraft, being an inseparable companion of Idolatry, Adulterers are taken for Idolaters in a Spiritual sense, and the false Prophets that used these Incantations to seduce the people are spoken of, vers. I, II; I3. who being false Prophets, or Witches, had defiled the Land with their several seducing Witchcrafts, leading the people to Idolatry, and in this practice of Charming Execrations, they were seducers of the people to repose confidence in ungrounded, and unwarranted composures of words to bring things to pass, which words so composed are meer Incantations, or Charms. In this Sixth description of a Witch in the text, or under the term of a Charmer, is contained Conjurers, who are Witches only in this sense, That they pretend that by vertue of words they can do many things, and amongst the rest, that they can by vertue of words command the Devil, which yet is but a meer cheating delusion to deceive poor Idolatrous people, who do more credit the vertue of words than they credit the truth of GodsWord; which foolish practice is sufficiently confuted, Acts 19. 23. certain Exorcists, or Conjurers, did take upon them to name over them that had evil Spirits, the name of the Lord Jesus, saying, I adjure you by Jesus whom Paul preacheth, and the Evil Spirits answered and said, Jesus I acknowledge, and Paul I know, but who are yee? Paul and the rest of the Apostles did indeed cast out Devils in the Name of Jesus, but not by the bare naming of Jesus, but by the spirit and power of Jesus; but if words could have done it, then those Conjurers might as well have done it, and then every one that could but imitate the Apostles, and the Prophets, and speak the same words, or the like, might work Miracles, but God will have it known otherwise, as appeareth in this place of the Acts aforesaid, That no words spoken, but the power of God bringeth things to pass. This was the manner of Idolatrous Heathen, to repose great confidence in Charms, and they that studied this practice of making and composing of Charms to seduce the people to this kinde of Idolatry, were Witches, according to this Sixth description in the text, Utens incantatione. If we do but read of the Heathen, we may fee in many places how they Idolized Charms, or

Incantations. Plutarch saith, That Aganice the Daughter of Hegetoris Thesali being skilful in the course of the Planets, foretold to certain credulous people an Eclipse of the Moon, and they had such confidence in Charms, that when they saw it came to pass, they beleeved that Aganice had with Charms plucked the Moon from heaven. Like to that in Virgil, Eclog. 8. Carmina vel Cælo possunt deducere Lunam, Carminibus Circe socios mutavit Ulyssis, Frigidus inpratis cantando rumpitur anguis. Inchantments pluck out of the Skie The Moon, though she be placed high; Dame Circes with her Charms so fine, Ulysses Mates did turn to Swine; The Snake with Charms is burst in twain, In meadows where she doth remain. Notwithstanding the Prophet David telleth us, That the deaf Adder heareth not, or regardeth not the voyce of the most skilful user of Charms, Psal. 58. 5. where he alludeth (with deriding) to the vain conceit of the Heathen, who reposed such confidence in Charms, and imputed such power to words. This Heathenish Witchcraft to cause people thus to Idolize Charms, is still practised by the Pope and his Train, their whole form of Religion, both in publike worship and common practice, consisting of Charms of all sorts, and of that very specifical difference of Incantation or Charming, which is called Conjuring, and if we look in the Masse-book, and if you search Durandus, you may finde Charms abundance, and he that is loath to take so much paines, let him but look Mr. Scots discovery of Witchcraft, the twelfth Book, the ninth Chapter, and so forwards, where he hath neatly set forth the Witchcraft of the Pope, and his Train, in the manner of their several Charms (though not exemplifying the tenth part of them) I will also shew you three or four of them, which Master Scot hath also rehearsed, with many more. The first shall be the Amulet that Pope Leo said he had from an Angel, who did bid him take it to a certain King going to Battel, and the Angel said, that whosoever carried that Writing about him, and said every day three Pater nosters, three Avies, and one Creed, shall not that day bee conquered of his enemies, nor be in any other danger ghostly or bodily, but shall be protected by vertue of these holy Names of Jesus Christ written, with the four

Evangelists, and the Crosses between them. + Jesus + Christus + Messias + Soter + Emanuel + Sabbaoth + Adonai + Unigenitus + Majestas + Paracletus + Salvator noster + Agiros Iskiros + Agios + Athanatos + Gasper + Melchior + and Balthasar + Matthaus + Marcus + Lucas + Johannes, Another Charm of Pope Leo sent to a King, having the like vertues in it, being read or carried about a man (being in an Epistle written by St. Saviour in these words.) The Cross of Christ is a wonderful defence + The Cross of Christ be always with me + The Cross is it which I do always worship + The Cross of Christ is true health + The Cross of Christ doth loose the bands of death + The Cross of Christ is the truth and the way + I take my journey upon the Cross of the Lord + The Cross of Christ beateth down every evil + The Cross of Christ giveth all good things + The Cross of Christ taketh away pains everlasting + The Cross of Christ save me + O Cross of Christ be upon me before and behind me + because the ancient enemy cannot abide the sight of thee + The Cross of Christ save me, keep me, govern me, and direct me + Thomas bearing the note of thy Divine Majesty + Alpha + Omega + first and last + midst + and end + beginning + and first begotten + Wisdome + and Vertue + This is still a common practice among the Papists to carry Charms about them (to make them Shot-free) when they go to Warre, as also hath been found by experience in the late Irish Warres (before the Cessation of Arms proclaimed by King Charls) many of the poor Idolatrous Irish Rebels being found slain with Charms in their pockets, composed by the Popish Clergy, the Witches of these latter times.

Another to be said in time of Sickness; first, let the Party sprinckle himself with Holy Water, and then say this Charm following, Aqua benedicta sit mihi salus and vita. Let Holy Water be both life and health to me. Another to be said every day, and upon every occasion, as often as any danger or occasion shall be; first, let the party that would be blest cross himself with his finger, making a sign of the Cross three or four times, and then say these words, and then without doubt he shall be safe. Signum sancta crucis defendat me à malis præsentibus, præteritis, and futuris, interioribus and exterioribus. That is, The sign of the Holy Cross defend me from evils present, past, and to come, inward and outward. A Charm or Conjuration, or an Exorcism, whereby they make Holy Water in the Popish pontifical, In Ecclesic dedicatione. I conjure thee thou Creature of Water, in the name of the Father, and the Son, and the Holy Ghost, that thou drive the Devil out of every corner of this Church and Altar, so that he remain not within our precincts, which are just and holy. After these words spoken, say they, that Water so Conjured hath power and vertue to drive away the Devil, and with this Holy Water they use many several Conjurations to keep the Devil in awe; with it they Conjure him from their Churches and dwelling houses, from their meat and drink, and the very Salt upon the Table; and if it were not for their continual Conjurations, they make people beleeve the Devil would walk every where, and kill, and devour, and carry away; therefore they Charm and Conjure their Bells in the Steeple (which they also Baptize and name by the I name of some Saint or Angel, and after these Ceremonies, (say they) and after such holy names named over the Bells, and the name of some Saint or Angel given to each Bel, and written upon them, those Bells have vertue to drive away and clear the air from Devils every where within the sound of them, from whence was the first beginning of passing peals, that the Devils might not come near to carry away the Soul of the dying man (although our Church use (I confess) to ring such peals only to give notice to their Neighbours, who desire to see them, and to pray for them before their departure.) They also use Charms at Funerals, perswading people, that the Souls of the dead, and also their Bodies, would be carried away by the Devil, if it were not for their charming (of which foppery Bucan a learned Theologian reproveth them, Loco 24. Quæstione 16.) and so the poor Popish people are deluded, so long as they see not the Devil in an ugly shape, they think they are safe, and the Devil farre enough, whereas the Devil is no where more than in a Popish Charm or Conjuration; and yet Master Scot hath collected in his twelfth Book so many Popish Charms, as it appeareth they had Conjurations, and other Charms for the Plague, the Quartain Feaver, the Consumption, the Toothache, and all manner of Diseases in Men and Cattel; and it appeareth still among common silly country people, how they had learned Charms by tradition from Popish times, for curing Cattel, Men, Women, and Children; for churning of Butter, for baking their Bread, and many other occasions; one or two whereof I will rehearse only, for brevity. An old Woman in Essex who was living in my time, she had lived also in Queen Maries time, had learned thence many Popish Charms, one whereof was this; every night when she lay down to sleep she charmed her Bed, saying; Matthew, Mark, Luke, and John, The Bed be blest that I lye on. And this would she repeat three times, reposing great confidence therein, because (as she said) she had been taught it, when she was a young Maid, by the Church-men of those times. Another old Woman came into an house at a time when as the Maid was churning of Butter, and having laboured long and could not make her Butter come, the old Woman told the Maid what was wont to be done when she was a Maid, and also in her Mothers young time, that if it happened their Butter would not come readily, they used a Charm to be said over it, whilst yet it was in beating, and it would come straight ways, and that was this: Come Butter come, come Butter come, Peter stands at the gate, waiting for a buttered Cake, come Butter come. This, said the old Woman, being said three times, will make your Butter come, for it was taught my Mother by a learned Church-man in Queen Maries days, when as Church-men had more cunning, and could teach people many a trick, that our Ministers now a days know not. Thus we may see still how the Witchcrafts of that grand Witch, that Whore of Rome, hath deceived all people; yet I would not have any think that I accuse the old Wives for Witches, for they used these Charms not to seduce, but were seduced, and bewitched by them to repose confidence in them; but the Popish Rout, the contrivers of these Charms, to delude the people, were the Witches; those poor deluded old Wives were Idolaters, Idolizing of words.

A Devillish practice of Conjuring Charms used by the Popish Clergy, discovered at Orleance in France acted chiefly by two Popish Doctors in Divinity, Colimanus, and Stephanus Aterbatensis, and their Knavery found out. IN the place aforesaid, in the year of our Lord, 1534. it happened that a Maiors Wife dyed, and was buried in the Church of the Franciscans, her Husband giving the Popish Clergy only six Crowns at the Funeral, whereas they expected a greater Prey, and were much discontent; it happened shortly after, that as they were mumbling their Prayers in a Popish manner, according to their usual custom, in the Church, there was heard in a secret Wainscot over the Arches of the Church a great rumbling noyse, the Moncks with the said Doctors presently began to Conjure, and to ask if it were not some spirit of some body lately dead, and if it were, they conjured the same Spirit to rumble again by way of answer, which it did; then they charged him by their Conjurations to answer by rumbling and knocking whose spirit it was, they named many that had formerly been dead and buried, and the Spirit would not answer by rumbling and knocking when they named them; but at last to bring their purpose to pass, they named the Maiors Wife, and then the Spirit rumbled exceedingly, and made a fearful noyse, this they acted several times, that it might be known in the City, so that many people came to the hearing and witnessing of this strange Wonder; but at the last they by their Conjurations had made the Spirit so tame, as it made them answer by knocking to any thing they desired it should answer; always when it answered not by knocking, then they concluded the thing was not so as they asked, or demanded, but otherways when it knocked, then that was an affirmative to the thing asked; at last they made the Spirit confess by that manner of answering, That it was the departed Soul of the Maiors Wife, and that she was damned for holding the Heresie of Luther, and that she desired that her Body might be taken up again and buried in some other place, for that place was not fit for the body of the Damned, being a Consecrated place. But the Maior being wise, and full of courage, so handled the matter, that he with the help of some of the City that loved him well, caused the place to bee searched where the noyse was; the Moncks did take the matter grievously, and would have resisted, it being at a time of the holy Conjuring, but yet the Maior causing a search, found, there a young Boy, placed there by these Popish Doctors, on purpose to act the part of a Spirit, as formerly related, and upon examination he confessed the whole imposture, to the shame and confusion of the Actors and Contrivers thereof, who were by the Laws (which were then and there free notwithstanding the Popish Tyranny) censured to be carried to the place of Execution, there to confess their deluding Witchcraft. Let the Reader take special notice, that the Actors, and Contrivers of this notable peece of Witchcraft were Witches in a three-fold sense. First, In their bringing to pass their cheating imposture, by confederating with a young Boy to act the part of a Spirit, they were Juglers, according to the first term of description. Secondly, In their Charms and Conjurations, whereby they charged the Spirit to answer them, they were Inchanters and Conjurers, according to this Sixth term of description. Thirdly, In their consulting with the spirit of the dead, the Maiors Wife, they were Necromancers, according to the Ninth term of description. This Imposture may be paralleled with that of the Witch of Endor; from this cousening Witchcraft of the Popish true, our common Wizards have learned their craft of cousening the people, making them beleeve they can Conjure up the Devil to give them Oracles according to the matter that they seek to the Wizard to be resolved of, and can conjure him down again at their pleasure. As for example, I will give you a true story, but whether you beleeve it or not, it will serve to illustrate the manner of their deceivings. A Butcher in Essex having lost Cattel, hee resolved hee would go to a Cunning man, to know what was become of his Cattel, and so went to a notable cousening Knave, that was (as common people say) skilful in the Black Art, and this deceiving Witch, seeing his opportunity of gaining a Fee, for the purpose in hand, used his Conjurations in a room contrived for his usual impostures, and presently came in a Confederate of his covered over with a Bulls Hide, and a pair of horns on his head, the poor Butcher sitting and looking in a Glass made for that purpose, in which hee was to behold the Object more terrible, and not so easily discovered as if he had looked right upon it, for he was charged by the Conjurer not to look behind him, for if he did, the Devil would be outragious; this confederate, or counterfeit Devil, after the Conjurers many exorcising Charms, or Conjurations, willed the Butcher to look East and West, North and South to finde his Cattel; the Butcher sought much to finde his Cattel according to the Devils counsel, but yet perceiving after much seeking and not finding, that it was a meer peece of Knavery, returned to the Conjurer again, and desired him to call up the Devil once again, which he did as formerly, but the Butcher had appointed his Boy to stand near hand without the house with a Mastiff Dogge, and at the Butchers whistle, the Boy as he was appointed, let go the Dogge, which came in presently to his Master, and seised upon the Knave in the Bulls hide; the Conjure cried out, as likewise the Devil, For the love of God take off your Dogge, Nay, said the Butcher, fight Dogge, fight Devil, if you will venture your Devil, I will venture my Dogge; but yet after much intreaty he called off his Dogge, but wittily discovered the cheating craft of Conjuring. He that acteth the part as this Conjurer did, with the same intent to deceive, and to make silly people beleeve and repose confidence in words (that is, in Charms and Conjurations to command the Devil, and to keep him in awe) is a seducing Witch, as he was; but he that acteth the same part, and causeth people to wonder at him, and to think that hee hath really conjured the Devil, to this intent only to shew to the world in a sporting way, how easily people are and have been deceived, is no Witch, but may be an instructer and inlightner of silly people, according to the Fifth description of Jugling delusions, in Pag. 42. And truly (if people were not so much naturally given to vain credulity, or beleeving of Lyes) that sort of Conjurers (so commonly prated of by silly people) had not been heard of in the world, had not these deluders learned this cousening craft from the Popish rout, whereby they delude silly people, making them beleeve they do things really by vertue of words, as by the naming of the Trinity, and the several names of God, and of Christ, and by naming of Angels, Arch-Angels, and the Apostles (just the same with Popish Conjurations) whereas, their doings, as likewise the Popes, are all but cheating impostures, for if Conjuring Charms could keep the Devil in awe, why did hee not submit to the Conjurers, Acts 19. 13? Another notable true Relation of what happened in a Town in England, wherein is plainly shewed how easily men are deceived by Jugling Confederacy in Conjuration. IT happened, that a Minister being remote from his dwelling, lodged in an Inne, and because he wanted company fit for him, he sent for a young Cambridge Schollar to keep him company, who being of his acquaintance, and dwelling in the Town, came to him, and after some discourse they fell into a dispute about Witches, and their Power, the Minister affirming, That Witches do truly conjure up the Devil in several shapes as they list, for said he, I know some that stood privately behind a Hedge when a Conjurer raised up the Devil in the shape of a Cock, and then again in the shape of a Horse, and heard the Cock crow, and the Horse neigh, but being very dark they could not see him; but the Scholar holding the contrary opinion, said, I will undertake to demonstrate the same thing to you in this Chamber, so as you shall verily think that I Conjure up the Devil in such shapes; Come on said the Minister, if you can do that, then also will I acknowledge these things to be but delusions. Now mark how strangely it happened, There was a Tapsters Boy in the Inne at that time, who had by wanton custom gotten a faculty of imitating the crowing of a Cock, the neighing of a Horse, the barking of a Dogge, the quacking of Ducks, and the noyse of many several Beasts, in a very wonderful manner; the Scholar therefore, for the lively acting of the foresaid Delusion, went down, and instructed this Boy to bring up a Jugge of Beer, and to set it down by the fire, and then to convey himself under the Bed, and withall to act the part of all several Creatures as the Scholar should call for them by Conjuration; now when this Boy had so conveyed himself under the Bed, the Scholar did put out the Candle, and left no light in the Chamber but the obscure light of a dim fire, the reliques of an Ostree Faggot, and said to the Minister, Now will I make you beleeve that I Conjure up the Devil, Come Pluto, I have a Letter to be sent with all speed to the Pope, therefore I conjure and command thee to come speedily to me from the lowest pit, in the shape of a swift running Horse, that may carry this Letter with speed, and bring me an answer; then began the Boy to snort, and neigh, and stamp, very much resembling a wilde marwood Horse, in so lively a resemblance, as it made the Minister begin to look sad, and amazed; then said the Scholar, Now I have well considered the matter, thou art not a Creature swift enough for this business, therefore I conjure thee down again, and I command Pluto to come to me in the shape of a Grey-hound, Præsto, vade, jubeo, celeriter; then the Boy under the Bed barked, and howled so like a Dogge, as the Minister did more and more creep close to the corner of the Chimney, sighing very sadly. Then said the Scholar, I consider that thou art not swift enough for my purpose, therefore I command thee to return to thy place, and, send me up a Cock; then the Boy crowed so like a Cock, as, no ear should distinguish it from a natural Cock; then said the Scholar, Thou art not a Creature swift enough for my purpose, therefore I command Pluto to send me up a Duck; at that command the Boy did so lively act the quacking of Ducks, as a man would have thought that many Ducks had been in the room. Then began the Minister seriously to exhort and admonish the Scholar, saying, Verily thou art farre gone, certainly thou art farre gone in this craft, and many more words; at which so sad discourse, the Boy under the Bed burst out in laughter, and came forth and acted his part again openly, and made the Minister ashamed. Yet here it may be noted, that the Ministers phantasie was so farre deluded, that he would not be perswaded, but that he saw real Ducks squirming about the room, as he expressed. I say then, how little credit ought Ministers or other men to give to flying Reports, when they themselves may so easily be deluded? The setting of Spels is referred to this description, and is done only by confederacy with him that is spelled; who feigneth himself so Charmed, or spelled, that others who would be in like action of Theevery, might fear to come into that place to steal, because of the Spel. So much for the Sixth term of description in the text, Utens incantatione, that is, an Inchanter or Charmer. THe Seventh term of description of a Witch in the text, is Requirens Pythonem, that is, Pythonicus Sacerdos, according to the sense of Plutarch, De defect. Orac. one that seeketh out an Oracle, as did the Priests of the Idol Apollo, which was called the Oracle of Apollo; the fame practice was common to the Priests of all Idols, that were in request before the Idol Apollo (although indeed Apollo being the most famous of the latest Idols, hath more Histories and reports still extant concerning their practice, than all former Idols have) as Plutarch witnesseth, that in Bæotia there had been many Oracles, some whereof grew silent when their Priests dyed, and some grew out of request for want of subtilty in giving answers (and because the impostures grew so common that people knew them, and would not be deluded by them any more.) We read there of the Lebadian Oracle, and the Amphiaran Oracle, and also of an Oracle of Mopsi, and at Amphilochi, and many more; these had their several terms of appellation, according to the Language of the people adjacent, as the Lebadian Oracle was given in the Æolic Tongue, and had its peculiar appellation in that Language; and so the Oracle at Delphos was called by such appellations as came from the Greek and also from the Roman Language, as Pytho, and Python, and Oraculum, and Oracles used by the ancient Heathen, were by the Hebrews in their Language called Ob, which Oracles were only giving Divinations to the peoples inquiries, as when Ahasia sent to inquire of the god of Eckron, 2 King. I. 2. save only this word Ob in the text, which is translated Python, implieth, the imposture whereupon these deceivers upheld their Divinations, as followeth by and by. This is not to be understood that they that did seek to such Witches as gave Oracles, that they also were Witches, for these were only bewitched Idolaters, but they only were Witches in this term of description, that being sought unto by these deluded Idolaters, used such deluding impostures, whereby they made the people beleeve they sought out an Oracle

71

(that is, an answer to the inquiry of those Idolaters) either directly from their Idols, or else that they sought out an Oracle from the spirits of the dead, as did the Pythonist of Endor, in which sense also they were called Necromantists, that is, such as asked counsel of the dead, being the Ninth term of description, I Chron. 10. 13. Saulus consulere Pythonem quæsusser, Saul had sought to ask counsel of the Oracle, there Saul was an Idolater, and not a Witch; but she that sought out that Oracle for him from the dead, she was a deluding Witch. This description, or term of description of a Witch, hath a various manner of expression in the Scriptures, which is needful to be noted by the Reader, for in this text, Deut. 18. 10, 11. such a Witch is called Pythonem requirens, one that seeketh out an Oracle; and in Levit. 20. 6. there such a Witch is called Python, an Oracle-giver, in these words, Anima quæ converterit se ad Pythones and arioles ut scortando seetetur eos, and c. That soul that turneth himself after Oracles and South sayers, to commit Idolatry, in following them, shall be cut off; and in vers. 17. of the same Chapter, Uiri autem aut mulieres si erit ex sis Pytho, aut ariolus, omnius morte afficiuntor; If there shall be found either man or woman that is an Oracler, or a South-sayer, they shall be put to death. There is also a Marginal note of Tremellius worth noting, in these words, Qui Diabolicis artibus reliquos à Dei cultu and sui sanctificatione avocant; Those Oraclers and South-sayers, saith he, are such as by their Devilish deluding craft do lead others from the true Worship of God, and living holily. People so mis-led to Idolatry are spoken of in vers. 6. chap. 20. of Leviticus afore noted. And further, look I Sam. 28. 7. there such a Witch being of the female kinde, is called, Mulier Pythone prædita, A woman that hath the craft of Oracling, or seeking out an Oracle. And Acts 16. 16. there such a Witch is said to have [Greek omitted], the spirit of Oracling; Where Beza in his Latine translation saith in his marginal notes, that that spirit of Oracling was only an expression, alluding to the Idol Apollo, which was called Python, and gave answers unto them that asked, namely, by the Priests that belonged unto it, of which Idol the Poets feigned many things; so they that had the imposture of Divination, were said by the Heathen to be inspired by the spirit of Apollo, Plutarch de def. Orac. and in this place of the Acts St. Luke speaketh after the common phrase of the Heathen, because he delivereth the error of the common people, but not by what instinct the Maid gave Divinations, for it is certain that under the mask of that Idol, the Devil played his deluding pranks, and this spirit of Apollo was nothing, but as much as to say, an imposture, or deluding trick of the Devil, practised by the Priests of Apollo. So much saith Beza, who plainly expoundeth, that that spirit of Divination, or Oracling, was only a Devillish deluding imposture, and not a familiar Devil, as many do fondly imagine. And whereas it is said in the verse following, that Paul did cast that Spirit out of the Maid, it was, that he by the power of the Gospel of Jesus rebuked her wickedness, so that her Conscience being terrified, she was either converted, or else at the least dared not to follow that deluding craft of Divination any longer; as when Christ did cast out seven Devils out of Mary Magdalen, it is to be understood that he did convert her from many Devillish sinful courses in which she had walked, Luke 8. 2. and 7. 47. (But if any be still so obstinate as to follow the common fond tradition, that Python, or Spiritus Pythonis, was a real familiar visible discoursing Devil, yet I hope none are so mad as to say upon serious consideration, that it was any thing but a spirit of lying Prophecie, or Divination, or Oracling in all the discourse of the Scripture, no man can shew in all the Scriptures, be they never so grosly expounded, that any man or woman had a killing, or a murdering Devil, whereby to bewitch any man to death, nor the least colour of any such Devillish exposition.) This Seventh term in the text, namely, Requirens Pythonens, one that seeketh out an Oracle, differeth not from the second term of description, that is, Utens Divinationibus, one that useth Divinations, or false Prophecies, save only in this, that that second term of description implieth only bare Predictions of suture things, and telling of hidden things, by which the Witch was described, but this Seventh term of description implieth some particular impostures, whereupon the Witches grounded their Predictions; according to which impostures they are called Oraclers, or seekers out of Oracles; the Hebrew word is Ob, and is translated Python; Ob signifieth properly a Bottle, or any such like hollow thing; and here in the text, and in all other Scripture-sense it implieth the imposture of speaking with their mouthes in a Bottle, from a hollow Cave in the earth, out of which came a voyce, spoken by some confederate with the Impostor, or Witch, which confederate was upon such occasion to go into a secret conveyance, and to make answer to, the inquiry, with a hollow sounding voyce, caused by the Bottle, and so it seemed to the silly deluded people, that the, voyce came out of the firm ground, as an answer sent by the gods, by the departed soul of some Prophet, or other man that had formerly died (in which sense also they were called Necromantists, from asking counsel of the dead, being the Ninth term of description) for which imposture all Idol houses, and houses of all such other Witches as practised, the same imposture, that the Idol-Priests did practice, were built and contrived on purpose with a room called Manteum, in which the said Cave and hollow passage was, in which room some fond Writers do say, that the Devil spake, but had it been so, that a real familiar Devil had answered, as is fondly imagined, why then did he answer only in that room? Surely if their Devil was so familiar, and at command, he might as well have answered in any room as in that, but a confederate man or woman could not bring to pass the imposture in any room but in that. This imposture is alluded unto by the Prophet Isaiah 29. 4. Sitq; quasi Pythonis è terra vox tua, and è pulvere sermo tuns pipiat, and thy voyce shall be as an Oracler out of the earth, and thy speech shall be whispering out of the dust: because they used cheating impostures to seduce the people, making them beleeve they could call the departed Ghosts of their friends to give them Oracles, or answers to their inquiry, out of the earth, this imposture the Prophet Isaiah warneth the people to avoyd the delusion of it, Isaiah 8. 19. in Tremellius translation, Quum enim edicunt vobis, consulite Pythones and ariolos, qui pipiunt and mussitant; nonne populus Deum, suum consulturus est? pro viventibus mortuos consulat ? for when they say unto you, Ask counsel of Oraclers, and South-sayers, that whis per and mutter, should not a people ask counsel of their God? Shall they ask counsel of the dead for them that are living? And here in Isaiah 29. 4. the Prophet alludeth not to all the impostures of such Oracling Idols, which were many, but only to this one imposture, from whence they had their description, or term of appellation from speaking in a Bottle out of the earth. In this sense the Pythonist of Endor was called Mulier pythone prædita, a Woman indued with an Oracle, or with the imposture of Oracling, because she made it seem by the foresaid imposture, to silly, deluded, or bewitched people, that the dead spake out of the earth, by which imposture she deluded Saul, I Sam. 28. And because that History of the Witch of Endor hath been commonly mis-interpreted, and many unwary Readers do beleeve, that that which she did was somewhat more than a cousening imposture, and that she did either raise up Samuel, or the Devil in the likeness of Samuel, or assuming the body of Samuel, and speaking in it (where by the way it is to be noted, that if any such things were, it maketh nothing to prove the common error, that a Witch is any where at all taken for a Murtherer; for the scope of all that she did, was only at last to give an Oracle, or Divination to Saul) yet let but such a Reader as thinketh she did any thing really; examine well the Chapter, and he shall finde, it was only a deluding cheating imposture by a confederate in the ground, and he that will not beleeve this, let him but gather up his Objections, and I will lay down my Answers as followeth. The first Objection, or ground of mistake, is, the twelfth verse of the Chapter, I Sam. 28. And when the woman saw Samuel, and c. Here perhaps you wil say, it is plain she saw Samuel? Ans. It is not here to be understood according to the letter of the History, neither did yet any Expositor so understand it, for it may not be supposed that any Devillish Craft can call a Saint from Heaven; no, but you will say, It was the Devil in the likeness of Samuel; I answer, If you hold to the letter of the History, you must say it was real Samuel, but if you vary from the letter, whence then can you gather that it was the Devil? And why is not this Exposition true, that she only pretended that she saw Samuel, to bring about her cousening imposture? for I have made it plain in all the discourse of this Book by the current of the Scriptures, that all Witchcraft was only a delusion, and to say that it was the body of Samuel raised up by the Devil, is to make the Devil able to work the same Miracle that was wrought by Christ upon the Cross, who by the power of his God-head raised up the Bodies of the Saints, for a time, who appeared unto many, from whence the Centurion concluded, that Christ was the Son of God, knowing that no other power was able to do it, Math. 27. 52, 53, 54. The second Objection may be, she learned of Samuel that it was Saul, as in the twelfth verse, And when the woman saw Samuel she said unto Saul, why hast thou deceived me, for thou art Saul? therefore she saw him. Answ. The seeing of Samuel could instruct her nothing, if living Samuel had been there, much less dead Samuel, nor seeing the Devil in Samuels likeness, for neither the body of Samuel, nor the Devil, was a Looking-glass to see Saul in, but it was her subtill pretence, and colour, that she had seen Samuel, and so found out Saul by her craft, whom she knew before; think you that this subtill Wizard did not know the King? when she dwelt nigh the Kings Court, as appeareth in the Chapter, for he went thither and stayed while she acted her part, and after a while she prepared meat, and he and his Servants did eat, and returned the same night. But you may say, he was disguised. Ans. He was taller than all the men in Israel by the head and shoulders, and without making himself so much the shorter, he could not but be known by a subtill Wizard. Also I answer; That the Servants of Saul, that could so readily tell him where he should finde such a woman at Endor, could not but be intimate with her, and so warn her of Sauls coming or give her some discovery of the present occasion, at their coming along with Saul, or else how could they have concealed her, and kept her counsel in the time a little before, when Saul had made strict proclamation that all Wizards should be banished the Land, as they were, and doubtless had not those servants concealed her, she had also been banished. Again,

Saul could not but discover himself to her, by his Oath that he sware to her immediately before, for who was able to save her from punishment but the King. Another Objection is, Saul himself saw Samuel, or the Devil in his likeness. Ans. It is plain in the History, he saw neither Samuel, nor his likeness, for he said to the woman in vers. 13, 14. What sawest thou, and what form and fashion is he of? where it is plain, he was only too credulous, and beleeved that she had seen some apparition, for if he had seen any thing himself, why did he say, What sawest thou? She answered, I saw an old man cloathed in a mantle, making a true description of Samuel, because she knew that he was the man that Saul desired, then Saul acknowledged that it was Samuel, only from her describing of him, vers. 14. and therefore bowed himself with his face to the ground in honour to Samuel, whom he expected should answer him out of the earth. Another Objection is; But Samuel talked with Saul? Ans. It is proved before that Saul saw no body, therefore Saul only heard a voyce which he imagined came from Samuel, but was only the voyce of a Confederate under the ground. But you will say, that the Scripture saith, Samuel said unto Saul, Why hast thou disquieted me? Aus. If you hold me to the letter of the History, why do you not hold yourself to it, but say, it was the Devil in the likeness of Samuel, as that it was real Samuel you will not say, why not a Confederate then? and here indeed the History is set down only according to the apprehension of Saul, not discovering the imposture. But how should she describe a man so like Samuel? that is, an old man cloathed in a mantle? Ans. The only noted Prophet in Israel was known to all, and could not be unknown to a subtil Wizard, whose practice was to be acquainted with all things of note, the bettet to help her craft of Oracling Divinations upon any occasion for gain. Another Objection, But if it were not Samuel nor the Devil, what Confederate was able to tell Saul so right, and give so true an Oracle of what should betide Saul the next day in the battel? Ans. All such Oraclers and Wizards did give Oracles two ways. First, In doubtful things, they gave doubtful answers. Secondly, Where were more certain probabilities, there they gave more certain answers. Now what was more certain than that the Kingdom should be rent from Saul? Samuel had Prophesied of it, and all Israel knew it; and what was more probable than that the time was at hand, when so mighty an Host of his enemies were come against him, when his heart and spirit failed him, and when God had forsaken him? and if it had not come to pass, such Oraclers did use to have evasions, the fault might have been laid upon Samuels Ghost, and further cousenage might still have been wrought to blinde Sauls eyes; and had it happened how it could, so that the Witch had come off blewly, and her imposture been afterward known to Saul, yet she had the Oath of the King to save her harmless. Further, it is the opinion of some learned men, that there was no certainty at all in the answer given to Saul, and that it was meerly conjectural, and though happening some way true, yet it failed in the day prefixed, for whereas it was said, To morrow shalt thou and thy Sons be with me, vers. 9. it was very false, for when the Philistims went up to Battel, David returning was three days marching back to Ziglag, I Sam. 30. I. and one day pursuing his enemies, vers. 17. and the third day after that, tidings was brought to David from the Camp of Saul, that Saul and his Sons were dead, 2 Sam, 1, 2, 3, 4. which made in all seven days, and therefore it was not likely that Saul and his Sons were slain upon the morrow, which was the scope of the Oracle, or answer that was given to Saul; this I say, is the opinion of a learned Writer. So much by the way. Further, if it had not been a meer delusion to blinde the eyes of Saul, why must Samuel bee described an old man cloathed in a mantle? That indeed was the fashion of living Samuel, but after he was dead and buried, had Samuel appeared as she pretended, or had the Devil appeared in his likeness, as some fond Readers suppose he did, it must have been like Samuel in a Winding-sheet; but indeed had she described him by his Winding-sheet, that might have been any man else as well as Samuel, and Saul had not been so easily deluded in his fond credulity and Idolatrous way. If you think it an incredible thing that Saul should be so easily deluded, look I saiah 8. 20. in the Latine translation (which carrieth the true sense of the Original, how odly soever our English Translators run) where the Prophet speaking of such as would counsel men to seek to Oraclers and Southsayers, he saith (in Tremelius) An non loquuntur in sententians illam cuicunq; nulla est Incis scintilla; do they not give this counsel to such as have not the least spark of light or underftanding? and this was Sauls case, Saul indeed had been a wise man formerly, when the Spirit of God was upon him, when it was said, Is Saul also among the Prophets? but then when God had forsaken him, his wisdom, his courage, and his victoriousness went all away together, and then, and never till then, was he deceived by a Witch. And however many erroneous Readers, when they read this History of the Witch of Endor, do suppose she did such things really as are set down, only according to the apprehension of the Spectators (namely, Saul and his Servants) yet let them but consider the nature of impostures, and they may easily conceive how such a cheating imposture might easily, and still may be brought to pass to delude fools, by an ordinary Jugling confederacy, according to the manner afore described, as well and as really as ever she did it, and that without a familiar Devil (as is foolishly supposed she had) only a Devil ruling in the heart of them that do it to the like end, to delude and lead people from God, as she did, the Devil being the Father of all lying delusions, and ruleth in the hearts of the children of disobedience. Such a Devil was in the heart of Ahabs Prophets, I King. 22. 23. (But for such as will not allow of that exposition, that the Witch of Endor did all by a confederate, I say, she might do it also-by the imposture of Hariolating, as may beseen in the latter end of the Eighth term of description following) And truly, for such as will still beleeve the common foolish errour, that Python was such a Witch as had a familiar spirit (except they mean such a lying spirit of Oracling Divination) I wonder how farre they will stretch the sense and coherence of the Scriptures, to make any such interpretation? Look but Tremelius Translation, a Chron, 33. 6. it is said of Manasseh, among the Witchcrafts which he used (or rather that the Idolatrous Priests under him used) Instituitq; Pythonem; What is that? Did he set up a familiar Spirit? one that had a familiar Spirit; or did he set up an Oracle? Which is best sense? but the common conceit of Readers is, because their Dictionary saith Python signifieth a Devillish spirit of Divination, or one that hath such a Spirit, therefore that must needs be a familiar Spirit (and indeed the common abuse of words may make words signifie any thing) but let such as trust only to their Latine Dictionaries, or Greek Lexicen, shew me in them, or any authentique Writer, but especially in the Scriptures, where Python is taken in any such sense as a familiar Spirit, (especially where it is taken for a killing spirit of a Witch) according to the common doctrin of Devils, that hath defiled the Nations, but only for a spirit of lying Prophecie, or one that hath such a Spirit or Devil in his heart; and in the text it is taken for the Oracle of the Devil; and if any carp at words, yet they must examine as well the sense of the Original, and the sense and coherence of the Scriptures from place to place, as what words may by abuse and ill custom signifie; yet I say, where do we read of a Familiar Spirit in all the Scriptures, if they be truly translated, especially where do we read of a killing spirit of a Witch? So much for the Seventh term of description, Requirens Pythonem. The Eighth term of Description. THe Eighth term of Description of a Witch in the text, is, Ariolus, for the most part written Hariolus, and is by all men taken for a South-sayer, but a South-sayer differeth not from Utens Divinationibus, being the Second term of description, for what difference is there between South-saying, and using of Divinations, or lying Prophecies? so then it might seem to be a Tautologie in the text; but as it hath been said before, that these Nine terms of appellation in the text, are not terms of distinction, but several terms of description, so if Moses had set here down a hundred several terms of description, signifying one and the same thing, it had not been a tautologie in the worst sense, but a more full expression of the same thing for illustration of the matter in hand: but yet as most of the rest of the terms of description in the text did all tend to Divinations (being the Second term of description) only they do imply a several imposture, whereupon the self-same Witches grounded their Divinations, and yet being described by their several impostures were not so many several kinds of Witches, but still one and the same kinde, and all of them false Prophets, who by several impostures seduced the people; so it may well bee understood, that under this Eighth term of description in the text, Hariolus, commonly called a South-sayer, is implied some particular imposture used in their Divinations, whereby to delude and seduce the people, which imposture, though it be not fully declared in the Scriptures, what it was, yet it may be collected by the several places in the Scriptures where the said expression is so often repeated, that it was some imposture used, together with the foresaid imposture of Oracling, (being the Seventh description) because in most places of the Scripture, Pythones and arioli are named together as one and the same, although implying a several imposture. The Hebrew word in the text is Jiddegnoni, or as by some pronounced Jiddoni, and signifieth Hariolus, but the Hebrews borrowed a word from some other Language, which word is Hartumim, which in Gen. 41. 8. 24. and in several places of Scripture, is used as a general word for all sorts of Witches, and is by Tremelius translated Magus, a Magician, but by common use did signifie among the Hebrews, Hariolus, a South-sayer, and yet used equivocately to express the Genus, and the Species as one, because South-sayers were Magicians, and were counted the only wise men, and is by many Expositors expounded Hariolus. The Latines commonly used another word, Haruspex; and here it may be noted, that these words, Hartumim, Hariolus, Haruspex, do imply the imposture of a hollow feigned voyce, which those Witches or Deceivers used in their Oracling Divinations, by harring in their throats, and these are they that are also otherwise called Pythones, according to another imposture of speaking in a Bottle, as in the Seventh term of description is before thewed Plutarch; de difec. Orac. saith, They that used to draw a Prophesying voyce out of their belly are also called Pythones, that is, as Johannes Scopula upon the place of Plutarch, saith, [Greek omitted] e ventre Hariolantes, and this was the imposture aimed at in the text under the Eighth term of description, Ariolus, namely, that they spake with a counterfeit voyce of harring in the throat, whereby to dissemble some other, and therefore changed their Natural voyce, and these were they that spake in the room of the Idol Houses, called in Greek and Latine Manteium (as in the Seventh description) and these were they that speaking in that room in a Cave under the ground, or some other hollow place, did therefore change their natural voyce, to counterfeit the voyce of some other; such a one was he that being confederate with the Witch of Endor, feigned the voyce of Samuel talking to Saul (as is more fully set down in the Seventh term of description) or she her self might by this Imposture speak all that was spoken to Saul; and these did rather har in their throats, that they might thereby the more terribly dissemble a voyce from the dead rising again, and therefore differed as much as they could from Human voyce; such a one was also by the Græcians and Latines called Mantes, which some Writers that knew not the imposture, say it was the Devil; but Mantes was such a Witch, or false Prophet, as had that devillish imposture of harring in their throats to deceive the people, called of some Ventriloquium, a speaking in the belly, and they that practised this imposture were so perfect in it, that they would speak so strangely, that many times they dared to practice their imposture above ground, whereby they made it seem to silly people that the spirit of Apollo, or some other Idol (which they called gods) spake within them, according to the expression of Saint Luke, who used the vulgar expression, Acts 16, 16. where it is said, the Maid had Spiritus; Pythonis, the spirit of Oracling, or as Beza expounds it, the spirit of Apollo, which he saith was only a devillish cousening imposture (as is before noted at large in the Seventh description) And this exposition of Ariolos is agreeable to the saying of the Prophet, Isai. 8. 19. Quum enim edicunt vobis consulite Pythones and ariolos, qui pipiunt and mussiant; and when they say unto you, Ask counsel of Oraclers, and South-sayers, that peep, and that mutter, here Tremelius gives this Exposition; The Prophet (saith he) aggravateth the heinous crime of these Witches from the vanity of those Divinations, which the very manner of them betrayeth, those Seducers have not so much wit that they dare speak to the people the thing they pretendu to speak in plain and open terms, with an audible cleer voyce, as they that are Gods Prophets, who speak the Word of God as loud as may be, and as plain as they can to the people, but they chirp in their Bellies, and very low in their throats, like Chickens half out of the shels in the hatching. So much Tremelius. And further he saith, That many Historians do mention these their delusions, but especially Origenes advers. Celsum. This imposture of speaking in the Belly bath been often practised in these latter days in many places, and namely in this Island of England, and they that practise it do it commonly to this end, to draw many silly people to them, to stand wondring at them, that so by the concourse of people money may be given them, for they by this imposture do make the people beleeve that they are possessed by the Devil, speaking within them, and tormenting them, and so do by that pretence move the people to charity, to be liberal to them. Master Scot in his Discovery of Witchcraft, Lib. 7. Cap. I. writeth of such a one at Westwel in Kent, that had so perfectly this imposture of speaking in the Belly, that many Ministers were deceived by her, and made no question but she had been possest by a tormenting Devil, and came and talked so long with that Devil, and charged him in the name of God to go out of her, as that he said he would kill her, he would tear her it peeces; he would kill them all; He also told them whom sent him in, and accused some poor people for Witches. The words and testimony of this Devil were taken in writing, and how many they that sent him had Witched to death, and yet when this matter came to examination by two wise Justices of the Peace, Mr. Thomas Wotton, and Mr. George Darrel, the Maid being discreetly examined, confessed the whole imposture; and for confirmation of the truth of the matter, so plain was the Maid in confession, that she acted the same thing over again before the said Magistrates, and many other Gentlemen and Gentlewomen, to the shame of those Ministers who had taken the testimony of the Devil against poor people in writing, and were credulous therein, beleeving and teaching such Doctrins, that a Witch can send a Devil to possesse and torment people, and another Witch can cast him out; but if they and all Ministers were led by the Spirit of truth, they should know, that this deluding Hagge was the Witch, and not they whom she accused; for what difference was there between her imposture and a spirit of Divination? like the Maid, in Acts 16. 16. formerly mentioned, whose spirit of Divination or Oracling was only a Devillish cousening imposture, saith Beza; and such ought to be put to death by the Law of Moses, because they use Divinations, pretending the discovery of Witches, it being manifest therein that they are the Witches, and because they by false accusation murther others; such a Maid was lately at Brantree in Essex, who practised the same imposture to the astonishment of many, and gained mony from the deceived beholders, until the report thereof grew stale, and fools had done wondering, and thé concourse of people ceased, and her gains came not in, and then the Devil did easily leave her, and the business almost forgotten, and yet no men so ready to put in execution the Law of God against her, or any such, as against poor people that are accused by such, and by fools, and hanged up without ground or warrant, or possibility of truth. This imposture hath wrought strange delusions among the ancient Heathen, and the actors thereof did by this imposture delude the people; one way very notable was (by their speaking in the Belly in the manner aforesaid) they would make it seem to the Standers by that a voyce came from afar off, or from some secret place, and that that voyce was the voyce of some of the gods, and then they would report abroad that in such a place a voyce was heard, declaring, or commanding such and such matters, and the poor deluded standers by would witness, and report the same to be true, whereas the voyce came only from the deluding Witch that was among them when they heard the voyce; as we may read in Plutarch de defec. Orac. A certain ship sayling by the Island of Paxis (in which ship were some Ægyptians, the manner of which Nation was to practise the several impostures of Witchcraft, for their advantage and fame among the people) there was heard from the shore of Paxis a voyce, calling thrice to Thamus by name, (he being an Ægyptian in the ship) Thamus, when thou comest to Palos, report that great Pan is dead, which thing he did. When he came near Palos he looked toward the shore, and cryed aloud, Great Pan is dead; then there was heard a terrible sighing and groaning, which much affrighted the people in the ship; the report of this was speedily testified at Rome, in so much that this Thamus was sent for by Tyberius Cæsar, and so was much taken notice of in the Emperours Court; and although many were deluded by that voyce, which was so heard by the men in the ship, and did much dispute about it what it should signifie, yet they that do rightly understand the imposture of Hariolating, or speaking in the belly, may easily conceive that Thamus himself was the man, or some confederate with him, that spake the voyce, and made that mighty groaning at the last, thereby to delude the people, and to make himself famous, as some great Man, to whom some of the gods had spoken; and whereas it was about the time that Christ was Crucified, And some would have it that that voyce was really spoken by some strange Spirit, and might signifie Christ: I yeeld thus farre, that Thamus himself might have heard the fame of the passages of the Life, and Death, and Resurrection of Christ, and might speak of, and concerning Christ, not that he beleeved in Christ, but would tell some notable thing in his own deluding way, for the magnifying of himself among the people, implying, that he was the man to whom such a voyce should come from the gods; and whereas he said, Great Pan is dead, it was because the Jews were the posterity of Shepherds, and the Heathen had feigned Pan to be the god of Shepherds; thus might he mean Christ, as the Maid in the Acts, ch. 16. 16. acknowledged Paul and his Doctrin, not by belief, but thereby to uphold and countenance her imposture among the people, for her own fame and gain; so might this Impostor mean Christ; although, nor he, nor any other, did ever conclude any thing fully concerning the meaning of that voyce, but left it doubtful (as all Oracles of the Heathen were) insomuch that some told Tiberius, that it was spoken from the gods of one that was risen up between Mercury and Penelopa. Thus did Thamus by his imposture get himself fame at the Emperours Court (which was the thing he aimed at) and left superstitious fools disputing of an ambiguous Oracle. It hath been credibly reported, that there was a man in the Court, in King James his days, that could act this imposture so lively, that he could call the King by name, and cause the King to look round about him, wondring who it was that called him, whereas he that called him stood before him in his presence, with his face toward him; but after this imposture was known, the King in his merriment would sometimes take occasion by this Impostor to make sport upon some of his Courtiers; as for instance, There was a Knight belonging to the Court, whom the King caused to come before him in his private room (where no man was but the King, and this Knight, and the Impostor) and feigned some occasion of serious discourse with the Knight; but when the King began to speak, and the Knight bending his attention to the King, suddenly there came a voyce as out of another room, calling the Knight by name, Sir John, Sir John, come away Sir John; at which the Knight began to frown, that any man should be so unmannerly as to molest the King and him; and still listning to the Kings discourse, the voyce came again, Sir John, Sir John, come away and drink off your Sack; at that Sir John began to swell with anger, and looked into the next rooms to see who it was that dared to call him so importunately, and could not finde out who it was, and having chid with whomsoever he found, he returned again to the King; the King again had no sooner began to speak as formerly, but the voyce came again, Sir John, come away, your Sack stayeth for you; at that, Sir John begun to stamp with madness, and looked out, and returned several times to the King, but could not be quiet in his discourse with the King, because of the voyce that so often troubled him, till the King had sported enough. So much for this Eighth term of description of a Witch in the text, Ariolus a South-sayer. The Ninth term of Description. THe Ninth term of Description, is, Necromantis, a Necromancer, that is in the sense of the Hebrew, Consulens mortuos, one that seeketh counsel of the dead, as Tremellus noteth in the margent. This is the last term set down by Moses, in the text, describing a Witch, and this term implyeth the pretence in the impostures used by the foresaid Oraclers, and South-sayers, as in the Seventh and Eighth description (is amply set down); and that the world might fully understand the delusion of Witches, Moses here setteth down this last and more full expression, or term of description of a Witch, Necromantis, which is all one with the former, and in regard of Predictions was called in the Second description, Utens Divinatione, a Diviner; in regard of the imposture of giving Oracles from a hollow Cave in the earth, with a Bottle, was called Oh in the Hebrew (translated Python by Tremellins) that is, an Oracle, or an Oracler, according to the sense of Plutarch, de defect. orac. and in regard of the imposture of counterfeiting a voyce of another by harring in their throats, was called, Ariolus, or Hariolus; in regard of the asking counsel of the dead was called, Necromantis, or consulens mortuos, one that asketh counsel of the dead; and in regard of the Charms and Conjurations that they used, in calling up the souls and spirits of the dead, they were Charmers, or Conjurers. The Seventh and Eighth terms of description do imply the impostures which these deluding Witches used in their Oracling Divinations; this Ninth term of description implieth their pretence which they had in those cousening impostures, that is, they pretended that they consulted with the souls of them that were departed this life, and thereby could tell things to come, or things hidden; and this was one pretence of all that were Oraclers, or South-sayers, according to which pretence they were called Necromancers, according to that place in Ifa.. 8. 19. (very fitly rehearsed again in this description) in Tremellius translation; For when they shall say unto you, Ask counsel of Oraclers and South-sayers, that whisper, and that mutter, should not a people ask counsel of their God? shall they ask counsel of the dead for them that are living? And this pretence of these Witches is manifest, not only in the Scriptures, but in common Wrlters, where we may read the Tenents, and the Opinions of the Heathen concerning this matter, Plutarch de defec. orac. sheweth their opinions and vain conceits, That the souls of men that were departed this life, were of more excellent perfection, than the souls of men in the prison of the body; and these were by those vain Heathen called Genii, which Genii or departed souls (say they) being of such perfection, and having likewise familiarity with the gods, would (when they were sought unto by men living here) come and inspire them to give Divinations, which they could easily do, by reason of their perfect estate after this life. These were by some of the Heathen called, and esteemed gods, and were among the Romans called Manes, that is, Infernal gods, or souls of men, to whom they offered Sacrifices, called Inferiæ. The Pythonist, or Witch of Endor did act her part so subtilly, that she did not only pretend inspiration from the Soul of Samuel, but (to satisfie Sauls infatiable blindness in his demand) that she could call him up, and make him appear to her, both Body and Soul united again, to prophesie again to Saul; which thing indeed was acted by her according to the silliness of Sauls demand, as appeareth more fully in the Seventh description, who, after the Spirit of God had forsaken him, was given over to beleeve such foolish fancies of faithless and ignorant people, as silly Women, and Children, and fools are inclined to beleeve unto this day, that people after their death can walk, and frequent the Houses, and Gardens, and Orchards, where they have used to be in their life time, which thing is a meer fancy of faithless and ignorant people, and cannot be brought to pass by either Witch or Devil, either really, or in appearance; for it was a Miracle once done by the power of Christ at his suffering upon the Cross that many of the bodies of the Saints than were departed rose, and appeared unto many in the holy City, Mat. 27, 52, 53. from whence the Centurion acknowledged Christ to be the Son of God, knowing that such things could not be done but by the mighty power of God; and he that readeth over the foresaid Book of Plutarch, shall easily finde, that one of the chief grounds of Oracles and Divinations, was this vain conceit of the Heathen, that wanted the light of the Scriptures, that the souls of dead men did give answers to them that had knowledge in the Art of seeking of Oracles; which Art indeed was only a craft of working impostures to delude the people, as is set down more at large in the Seventh and Eighth descriptions; and from this old conceit of the Heathen, and practice of these deluding Witches of ancient times, hath that grand Witch, that Whore of Rome (the Pope and his train) derived her notable Witch-craft, whereby she hath deluded the world, teaching people to invocate the souls of Saints departed, as likewife to conjure them. Let but the Reader look back to the Sixth term of description (a Charmer) and there he may read of a notable peece of Necromancy acted by two Popish Doctors at Orleance in France, with their devillish Conjurations. These Roman Witches are the Necromancers of these latter Ages, according to this Ninth description; these are the Inchanters of these latter Ages, as is fully demonstrated in the Sixth description; these are the Jugling Witches of these latter Ages in the Christian world, as is fully demonstrated in the Fifth description, and therefore it is said of this Purple Whore, Revel. 18. 23. with thy Witchcrafts all Nations were deceived. And he that will be zealous for God, in obeying the command given in Exod. 22. 18. Suffer not a Witch, to lives must leave his fond ignorant course of teaching people to hang up poor, and widows, and aged, and lame helpless people, and must bend his devotion against that Whore of Rome (as all the world ought to do) as also against the Mahometan Witches among the Turks. Therefore it were a good Law in England, if duly kept, That no Jesuite, or Popish Priest should be suffered to live, in any part of these Dominions, because these Witches are they that bewitch the people (where they be tollerated) by their several deluding impostures, leading the people to Idolatry, and also to the undermining of Governments. So much for the Ninth term of description of a Witch in the text, a Necromantist, one that asketh counsel of the dead. The false Prophets of ancient times having their several impostures and pretences, whereby they seduced the people to vain Idolatry, which was abominable to Gods eyes, are here by the Spirit of God demonstrated to the world by the Nine several terms of description in the text, that the world might fully know the mystery of iniquity, and avoyd all such evil workers, as deceivers of his people, and learn to know God, and his Prophets, who teach people the right way of God; and these are the terms of expressions that are used in the Old Testament to demonstrate false Prophets, according to which expressions wee use the general word Witch, or Sorcerer, in the English Tongue, and do finde no other sort of Witches spoken of in the Scriptures. What sort of Witches soever are spoken of in the New Testament, are all taken in the same sense that they are in the Old Testament, and are sufficiently glossed at the beginning of this Book, upon the Definition of a Witch, and Witchcraft; but yet in Revel. 22. 15. there is found a word that is used as a general expression for all sorts of Witches, which word because it hath been abused by some Popish Expositors, and blinde interpreters, disputing upon the same word used by the Septuagint, it may not be omitted to speak somewhat of it, the word is [Greek omitted], signifying by Etimology a Poysoner, or a compounder of Poysons, and is tranflated veneficus, signifying also a Poysoner, and yet both words both in Greek and Latine are used commonly for a Witch in general of all sorts, and is so taken in that place of the Revelations, and from hence some that are willing to uphold fond Opinions, do draw this fond conclusion, That a Witch is such a one as killeth people by Poysons, and can infect the Air, and bring many mortal Diseases by Witchcraft, and by the same craft can kill any particular Man or Beaft with looks, by poysoning the Air in a direct line, as some feign of the Cockatrice. But what Logician will not say it is an absurdity to draw a Conclusion, and ground an opinion, from the bare signification of words? and yet for the words, it is easily conceived, that a Witch was first called [Greek omitted] in Greek, and Veneficus in Latine, by a Metaphor taken from the deceitfulness of a Poysoner, that giveth a man Poysons by deceit to betray his life; or from a deceitful Apothecary, or Mountebank, that selleth Pyson, sophisticated Medicines, instead of wholsome Physick, as a Witch is taken in no other sense in all the foregoing places of Scripture than for a

Deceiver, or Impostor; yet because (as I have said before) that bare significations of words do prove nothing directly, therefore let us but expound Scripture by Scripture, and we may easily finde that [Greek omitted], Veneficus, is taken for a Deceiver, or Impostor, and not for a Poysoner or Murtherer, and for that look Revel. 18. 23. With thy Witchcrafts all Nations were deceived; there the conjngal word is [Greek omitted] veneficiis tuis, as much as to say, with thy poysoned Medicines, or Poysons, all Nations were deceived; there is the same Metaphor used again, and such words as might signifie Poysons are used for deceiving Witchcrafts; with thy Witchcrafts all Nations were deceived, not killed. So then, to conclude with Revelations, we read not in all the Old or New Testament of a Killing Witch, or Murthering Witch, but only of deceiving Witches, Impostors, or false Prophets, seducing people to Idolatry by their delusions and impostures. He that will have any further description of a Witch, let him take this description; A Witch is as like a Prophet as can be, and yet a deceiving false Prophet, Dan. 2. 13. A Decree went forth from the King, that the Magicians should be slain, and they sought Daniel and his fellows to be slain; there the Executioners knew no difference between the Magicians and Daniel, that was a Prophet, for the word Magician, or Wise men, being properly taken in a good sense, was equivocally given to South-sayers, and all sorts of deceiving Witches, as well as to those that were termed Wise men, and as to the Prophets themselves, and under that Decree Daniel himself had been slain, if it had not been stayed by Gods providence. The blasphemous Priests and Pharisees called Christ a Deceiver, or Impostor, or as Beza expoundeth, a Jugler, and a Seducer, Matth. 27. 63. when as he was the great Prophet of the world. Plutarch saith, De defect. Orac. That he which first began the Oracle of Apollo was Coreta, who set up the Oracle, in a pretence of being Divinely inspired with the spirit of Prophecie. Mr. Scot in his Discovery, who (was a Student in the Laws, and learned in the Roman Laws) sheweth, Lib. 11. Cap, 5. and 6. that certain Colleges were erected at Rome, in time of Heathenish ignorance, for Diviners and South-sayers to be instituted to expound the mindes and admonishments of the gods, and by their Law young Princes were to be sent to Hetruria to learn, and bring home the cunning of that Art (it being the only Divinity the poor Heathen knew, to seek to such as pretended they could know the mindes and wills of the gods) and in process of time these Colleges increased to a great University, in which were brought up such as learned the practice of Divination, or Augury, by several impostures described in the text; who notwithstanding they were accounted Prophets among the Heathen, yet are all aimed at, and described in the text for Witches, and South-sayers, and such as the people of Israel (being a chosen people, to be taught by God and his Prophets) were commanded to destroy, that no such bewitching false Prophets should be found among them; such a one was Elimas the Sorcerer, called both a Sorcerer, and a false Prophet, Acts 13. 6. and these were such as were sometimes great Scholars, yet abusing their learning. Some may object and say, If Witches were only false Prophets, then all false Teachers are Witches? Answ. A Witch and a false Prophet are reciprocal terms, but not a Witch and a false Teacher, for all the Nine terms of description in the text are plainly describing Witches and false Prophets as one and the same, and having one of these two properties; First, He setteth up an Idol, which is the first main Witchcraft, being the first description in the text; or, Secondly, He useth some, or all of the eight following Witchcrafts described in the text, either to confirm and uphold his Idol by seducing the people, or else to make the people beleeve that he is a true Prophet of God, as did Simon Magus in the Acts, and as is rehearsed in the same Chapter in the text, Deut. 18.20. for the more full and general description of a Witch, or false Prophet, which was described in the text, by Nine specifical descriptions, specifying the Nine Witchcrafts of such seducing false Prophets: but yet it doth not follow that all false Teachers are Witches; for a man may be a false Teacher through weakness of understanding, and error of judgement (as were the Scribes and Pharises in some things) and yet not a Witch; but he that is a wilful upholder of Heresies, or any vain unprofitable Doctrin, only to draw people to a head to uphold his own gain, and so for gain maketh the people to miss of the sincerity of Religion, although he be no Impostor, nor bringeth himself within the compass of the punishment due to a Witch from the Civil Magistrate, because he doth not use impostures, or any of the Nine Witchcrafts described in the text, yet in his intent he maketh gain his end, and perverteth souls in a smooth pretence of holiness. I know not how his final intention differeth from the final intention of a Witch (that is, gain by seducing the people) nor whether he or a Witch shall have the greatest condemnation at the last day, Acts 20. 30. for it appeareth in vers. 20. following the text, that a false Prophet considered distinctly from the foresaid impostors, is in the same Condemnation, and the same with a Witch, and ought to be censured by the Civil Magistrate to dye as a Witch, meerly quatenus a false Prophet; for although he bee described by his several impostures before in the text, yet the bare using of impostures maketh not a Witch, unless by them he be a false Prophet; (as is demonstrated more fully in the Fifth description) so then, the Formalis ratio of a Witch, or that which maketh him to be a Witch, is, because he is a false Prophet, so that it followeth, that as every wilful false teacher, or wilful upholder of Heresie, or any vain unprofitable Doctrin to seduce the people for gain, differeth not in his final intention from a false Prophet, so by the same reason he differeth not from a Witch; and although he cannot always be convicted by the Magistrate, yet in Gods sight he is a very Witch. Our English Translators not knowing the difference of the terms of description in the text, by the several impostures therein implied, according to the intent and meaning of the Scriptures, have used words promiscuously one for another, without expressing the true and full meaning of the Original so well, as is exprest by Junius and Tremelius in Latine, as in Deut. 18. 10, 11. they call a Diviner a Witch, and a South-sayer a Wizard, expressing specifical descriptions by general words, that may be as well given to any of the nine; and in Exod. 22. 18. they call a Jugler a Witch, using the same general expression that they used before, for one that useth Divination, or a Diviner; they call a Planetarian an observer of times, a phrase more obscure than can imply the original meaning of the Scriptures; they call a Conjecturer an Inchanter, and they call an Inchanter a Charmer, where as in the Original and Latine Translations, an Inchanter, and a Charmer is all one term of description; they call an Oracler one that hath a familiar Spirit, and that may be as well given to any of the Nine terms in the text (by the same reason that all Witches have a familiar spirit, according to the common tenent, though it cannot be proved that any had any, otherwise than the spirit of error ruling in their hearts.) And 2 Chron. 33. 6. there they call using Divinations, observing of times, which phrase they used before for a Planetarian; and if we compare several English Translations, wee may finde them much varying one from another in translating of those terms, not but that they were good and able Linguists, but not knowing the several impostures implyed in these original terms of description, could not express them in such apt words in English, as if they had known the mystery of iniquity according to the original sense and meaning, Gen. 44. 5. they translate it, Is not this the cup by which my Master divineth? Here they would make Witchcraft lawful, (for Divination is Witchcraft) but the original sense is nothing so as they translate it; look Tremellius. All this argueth that these our ancient Bishops and great Clerks knew not what Witchcraft was in the Scripture sense.

The Second Book

It is manifest, that the Scriptures were given by God, for a rule for man in this depraved nature to walk by, That whereas all Mankinde since the fall of Adam are naturally darkned in their understandings, and averse from the truth of God, the Scriptures might be a light unto us, to lead us in the righteous way of Gods truth. And now Christ Jesus the Light of the World (in whom are fulfilled all the Divine Mysteries of the Scriptures) is come into the world to enlighten the world; and whereas before his coming the world sate in darkness, and were wholly given to run after Idols, and to be seduced by Idol-Priests, who practised the several Witchcrafts described in the text, Deut. 18. 10, 11. to seduce the people to Idolatry, yet then at the coming, and by the power of the coming of Christ, (who was manifested by Miracles, and taught the people by his Spirit of Truth) were all those ways of darkness discovered to the whole Word, to be lying delusions, tending to destruction, as is prophesied by the Prophet, Isa. Chap. 8. hee speaking of Witches, and their delusions, and the darksome errours and evils accompanying them, from the nineteenth Verse to the end of the Chapter, immediately in the two first Verses of the next Chapter, he prophesieth of Christ, the light of whose coming should destroy the ways of darkness, in these words, In the way of the Sea beyond Jordan, Galile of the Gentiles, the people that sate in darkness shall see great light, and upon them that dwell in the Land of the shadow of dealh shall light shine forth; and thus it was fulfilled at his coming. The Nations that were given to Idolatry, and seduced by false Prophets (being Idol-Priests, and deluding Witches) were so enlightned, that all Idolatrous delusions were discovered, the Oracle of Apollo, and of all Idols, grew dumb, Simon Magus, and Elim as the Sorcerer, and all bewitching false Prophets were confounded, and all these Instruments of darkness grew out of request among the people, being clearly discovered that they were all Lyars, and used lying delusions to deceive the Nations. And notwithstanding this

95

perfect rule of righteousness in the Old and New Testament, written by the Prophets before the coming of Christ, and at his coming finished by him and his Apostles, yet such is the obstinacy of mans darksome nature, that men will carry a Candle of their own in their hands, even at Noon-day, imagining they can by their own wisdom finde out truths that are not written in the Scriptures, and that their Candle will enlighten them more than the beams of the Sun when it shineth forth in its full strength; Like a silly Labourer, that counting the day by a Pocket Watch, whose Wheels being out of Kilter went too fast, he had such a conceit of his Watch, that he affirmed, That the Sun in the skie went too slow, for his Watch was known to be true. Thus do men play with the Scriptures, preferring Human traditions beyond the truth of God contained in the Scripture; and this is the cause why men a long time have been deceived by the Man of Sin, who still prevaileth to lead the World in darkness, because they love not the truth, but have pleasure in unrighteousness, 2 Tref. 2. 10, 11, 13. for this man of sin, that Whore of Rome, being the grand Witch of the Christian world, pointed at Revel. 18. 23. that hee might still have freedom to deceive the Nations, hath broached this Doctrin wherewith he hath defiled the world, that a Witch is not a false Prophet, or a Deceiver, but one that can send the Devil to kill men and women, and children, and to make the ground barren, and men and women barren in Generation, and kill the children in the Wombe, and can with looks kill Lambs and Cattel, and can fly in the Air, and can do many things by the help of the Devil; which things are not possible to be done by any power, but by the mighty power of God. We may read of the Priests of the Idol Astaroth, that were indeed real Witches in the Scripture sense, who professed to do such things by the power of their Idol, but were discovered by Bartholomaus the Apostle, to be deceivers of the people, by the Devils subtil delusions, who ruled in their hearts, so they with their Idol were destroyed, and many people converted to the Christian Faith. Hendor fius in the fifth page of his Theater of History (his words are these, Bartholomæus Idolum Astaroth evertit, fraudes Satan æ qui miraculis homines effacinatos morbis jampremebat, jam pressos levabat, detexit. and c..) And where do we read in Holy Writ (or common History that saver of truth) that men by Devils could do such things really? and to uphold such errours contrary to Scripture, what is this but meer prevarication with the truth, and resisting Gods holy Spirit of truth? Where do we finde any such thing in Scriptures, or any such description of a Witch, or that a Witch was such a one as hath made a League with the Devil, and sealed it with his bloud, or hath Imps sucking him, or Biggs, or privie Marks, or that lyeth with Incubus, or Succubus, or any such phrase or expression in all the Scriptures? What least inkling have we of these things in all the Scriptures? Whence received the Church of England this Doctrin? O foolish England, who hath bewitched you, that you should not obey the truth? Surely it was the Pope. This groundless, impious, and fantastical Doctrin was never taught by Gods Prophets, but that Witch, the Pope, knowing in his Conscience that he is the very Witch, the Deceiver of the Nations pointed at in the Revelations, and that the Scriptures were so plain, that by the light there of his devillish delusions must needs come to light, if the World should have true insight into the Scriptures, and so that by that means all Nations would rise up on him and-destroy him, he not only laboured to hide the Scriptures from the common people, which he did for a long time, but also hath been so bold as to prevaricate with the Scriptures, and to publish through the Nations, that Witches were to be understood no Deceivers, but such as practised such wonderful things, as the Scripture teacheth us that the doing thereof ought to be attributed to no Creature, but only to the Creator, as Pope Innocent the eighth to the Inquisitors of Alman, and Pope Julius the second, to the Inquifitors of Bergoman sent those words; It is come to our ears, that many lewd persons of both kinds, as well male as female, using the company of the Devils Incubus and Succubus, with Incantations, and Conjurations, do destroy the birth of Women with childe, the young of all Cattel, the Corn of the field, the Grapes of the Vine, the fruit of the Trees, Men and Women, and all kinde of Cattel, and beasts of the field, and with their said Inchantments do wholly extinguish, suffocate, and spoyl all Vine-yards, Orchyards, Meadows, Pastures, Grass, green Corn, ripe Corn, and all other provisions, men and women are by their imprecations so afflicted, with external and inward pains and diseases, that men cannot beget, nor women bring forth, nor accomplish the duty of Wedlock, denying the faith which in Baptism they profess, to the destruction of their souls; Our pleasure therefore is, That all inpediments that may hinder the Inquisitors Office be removed from among the people, lest this blot of Heresie proceed to defile them that be yet innocent, and therefore we do ordain by vertue of the Apostical authority, that our Inquisitors of high Almain may execute the Office of Inquisition, by all Tortures, and Afflictions, in all places, and upon all persons. What Scripture had the Pope for this? we read indeed of such Fictions in the Poets, as in Ovids Metamorph. 7. Cum volui ripis ipsis mirantibus ammnes In foxtes redire suos, concussaq; sisto, Stantia concatio cantu freta, nubila pello, Nubilaq; induco, ventos abigoq; veceq; Vipereas rumpo verbis and carmine sauces, Vivaq; saxa, sua convulsaq; reberaterra, Et Sylvas moveo, iubecq; tremiscere montes, Et mugire solum, manesq; exire Sopulchris, Te quoq; Luna traho. The Rivers I can make retire into the Fountains whence they flow, Whereat the banks themselves admire, I can make standing waters go; With Charms I drive both Sea and Cloud, I make it calm, and blow aloud. The Vipers jams, the rockie stone, with Word and Charm I break in twain, The force of earth congeal'd in one, I move the Woods, th' Hills tremble plain: I make the souls of men arise, I pluck the Moon out of the skies. Also Ovid, de Medea Epist: 4. Et miserum tenues in jecur urget acus, She sticketh also Needles fine, In livers, whereby men do pine. Also Virgil: Nescio quis teneros oculus mibifascinat agnos. I know not whence some fierce bewitching eye With looks doth kill my Lambkins as they lye. These are the Popes Scriptures whereon he groundeth his groundless inventions to torment the Christian World, and upon these grounds being inventions and pastimes of Poets, hath he sent out Inquisitors in all places to torment; from thence is the Spanish Inquisition, which maketh search for Hereticks and Witches all as one, and now lest the world should take notice that his daily practice is to torment and kill Reformists, and so his Villany ring the more in the ears of the world, he hath joyned as equivocal with the word Heretiques, Witches, a more ignominious name, thereby to instigate people the more against them, and so by this means will not be seen to kill men for matter of Religion, for then men would resist and help one another, but under the name of Witches he melteth away every one that hath but a smell of the reformed Religion, and the world perceiveth it not, this is that Grand Witch, the Whore of Rome, the Pope and his train. And these Inquisitors before mentioned sent out by the Pope, have for the confirmation of their villanous Doctrins and Inventions, set forth great Volumes of horrible lyes and impossibilities, and also for the hiding of their unparalleled cruelty from the ears of the world, of which sort are James Sprenger, Henry Institor, in malleo maleficarum, also Nider and Cumanus, Daneus, Hyperius, Hemingius, but most of all Bodlnus and Bartholomaus Spineus (I do not say that all these dyed Papists) and lest their authority should fail in deceiving the world in this Doctrin of Devils, some great Scholars of the Popish rout have approved and affirmed the matter to be true in some causes writing of fascination, and of that sort are Thomas Aquinas, and Suares. In which Authors (although they were learned men) whosoever readeth their discourse of this subject, shall finde nothing at all proved, either by Scripture or Philosophical argument, but they take it for granted and undoubted truth confirmed by tradition, that Fascination or Witchcraft is an Art of killing and afflicting Men and Cattel, and upon this Hypothesis they take in hand to dispute upon it, not whether it be true or not, but how it may be done, as they conceive, for say they, Et si agens non potest diffundere actionem suam usq; ad rem distantem, sit tamen ut aer proximus inficiatur and usq; ad certam distantiam perveniat, and sic noceat alteri; if this subject, the force of fascination had been first proved by them, then this their reason had had some seeming force in it, but because it can no way be proved by firm Argument, they quote History for it, and so pass on to their hypothetical disputes about the reason of it, and that they may make the matter seem true, one quotes anothers authority for it, and Suarex quoteth Thomas Aquinas and Pliny, and Pliny citeth Hogonus and Niphodorus, and Atollonides for his Authors, that among the Triballians, and Illyrians, and Scythians, there be certain Women that can kill with their eye-sight whom they look wishfully upon; mark, but how first things are reported by Travellers who may lye by authority; then Pliny gathereth their several reports into the Volume of his Natural History (whom all men may see was abused by being too credulous of other mens reports) and yet Suarez is forced to use Plinies Pen to prove that which cannot be proved or defended by reason, and having no better Argument, he saith further, Sunt qui negant illam vim fascinationis, sed non est cur experientiam à Philosophis and medicis comprobatans, and ferè communi sensu receptam, negemus; by which Argument a man may as well prove that Idols were gods, because they were approved in their time by men of all Arts and Sciences, Et ferè communi sensu recepta; and further (according to Plinies report) he saith, that these women do kill but by some poysonous quality of their Natural complexion, and inward humours of their bodies, communicated to the vital spirits, and by the action of the minde brought to the eye-sight, and from thence infecting the party whom they look upon, and this (he saith expresly) cometh naturally to pass, and of inbred natural causes in the Witches bodies; but mark how this fellow (although notable for learning) hath wildered himself in searching out the reason of a meer vain supposition, and erroneous tradition, that Witches can kill by looks; for whereas he giveth this reason, that Witches have inward natural poyson, whereby they naturally kill others; what an absurdity is this to say, that any Creature can by its natural quality be contrary or destructive to its own species? for a Viper cannot poyson a Viper, nor a Toad cannot poyson a Toad; for their nature is one, and not contrary to its own species. Secondly, whereas he reasoneth, that this poyson is communicated from the humours to the vital spirits, and by the action of the minde brought to the eye-sight. It is most absurd in Philosophy; for what Physician or Philosopher doth not acknowledge that the vital spirits, once poysoned, do suffocate the Heart, the fountain of Life (as is often seen in the Pestilence) whereby the Witch her self must needs perish; and is also often seen in those who having but the Natural humours of their own bodies corrupt, the vital spirits are debilitated, and cannot operate, but the party decayeth and soon perisheth, because the heart cannot abide any corrupt poyson, or contrary temperature to its own nature. Thirdly, whereas he saith, this poyson is sent from the Witch by the force of seeing, this also is an absurdity in Philosophy; for all sound Philosophers do acknowledge, that Oculus non vidit emittendo vim suam videndi ad objectum visibile, sed recipiendo species visibiles ab objecto; how then can the sight (if it were poyson) hurt any way the party upon whom it only looketh? Fourthly, whereas he saith, that Witches do kill by their natural complexion and inward humour, being naturally poyson, what an absurdity ariseth from hence in Divinity? To conceive that God should make men and women naturally poyson, and destructive to others, and yet should make a Law that such should be put to death, yea cruel death, for being such as God made them in their nature and complexion? Surely if man had stood in the manner in which he was made, God had not punished him with death. Now after he hath thus intrapped himself in his Discourse, by seeking out a reason of that which is not (but only conceived to be by credulous people) he falleth off from his own weak reasons, to the reason that Thomas Aqusnas giveth, and that is, That sometimes this Fascination is wrought by a secret compact with the Devil; but how can these Reasons accord one with the other? for if it be natural to the Witch to bewitch others, what needeth she then to seek help of the Devil to do that which she can do by nature? For, Deus est author Natura, and sure the Devil cannot make more perfect or forceable that which God hath made; but such is the nature of all these Popish Writers, that when they cannot strongly enough maintain a Lye, they father their Lyes upon their Master the Father of Lyes, and are forced, after all their vain argumentation, to use his name to uphold a Lye, and (although they were great Scholars) have rather intangled themselves with folly in reasoning, and with so manifest errour (whereby they have exposed themselves to the lash of common Censure) than to forsake their Popish darkness, which they are ingaged to defend. What shall not be done to bring the Popes ends to pass? what Lyes, what foolish Fictions, what impossibilities can the Heart of man devise, that these together have not affirmed for truth unto the World, to infect the Nations with Heresie, or Atheism, whereby to destroy the Christian Church? And for further confirmation of the matter, they have devised, among other Tortures, to make people confess that they can do such impossibilities, one of the most devillish cruelties that hath been devised among men, and that is, to keep the poor accused party from sleep many nights and days, thereby to distemper their brains, and hurt their fancies, at length to extort confession from them, and then to bring their own confession as an evidence against them; and if they cannot make them confess, they torture one of their little Children to make it accuse their Parents, and that they call confession; this trick will tame any wilde Beast, and make it tractable, or any wilde Hawk, and make it tame, and come to your fist, how much more may it make men or women yeeld to confess Lyes, and impossibilities? And if that device will not serve, then they shave them, and search narrowly all parts of their bodies, where they think modest men will not be forward to look, to see the truth of the matter, and there they report that they have found the Devils privie Marks, and Biggs, for the Devil to suck them; a most devillish Lye and invention, unless they can shew me Scripture for it, but I can shew them Scripture against it, Job. I.3. Without God was nothing made that was made; who then made those Biggs, or Teats, and who made the bodies of those Devils called Imps? Also what Scripture saith, that Biggs or privie Marks are signs or trials of Witches? (yet I deny not but sometimes are found fleshy Warts, and other preter-natural tumours written of by Physick Authors, as diseases of the body) and among other devices (as Master Scot in his discovery affirmeth (who was zealous for Gods truth, and took more pains than ordinary to search and confute those impious Writers) they have set down certain signs whereby to suspect and apprehend Witches, which are these; First, If they will not fast on Fridays. Secondly, If they fast on Sundays. Thirdly, If they spettle at the time of Elevation. Fourthly, If they refuse Holy Water. Fifthly, If they despise Crosses. Sixthly, If they deny any of the seven Sacraments. These are great suspicions that they are Witches; for the Devil (say they) chooseth them by these signs (being steps to the reformed Religion) apprehend them, bring them to the Tormentor; but if they see any of these signs, they will easily finde other holes enough in their Coates to condemn them. Then they cast them into the water, to see whether they will sink or swim, a meer Jugling delusion to blinde peoples eyes, for he that hath been used to the Art of Swimming may know, that few men or women being tied hand and feet together can sink quite away till they be drowned, or if he lay them flat on their back, and hold up their feet with a string, their fore-part will not sink, and therein they can use Jugling to blinde the peoples eyes for difference sake; for when they will save any man or woman, they will let loose the string which they hold in their hand, and let their feet sink first, and then all their body will sink, then they cry one to the people, Look you now, and see the difference betwixt an honest man or woman, and a Witch, take her out, she is an honest woman, yea verily, for sometimes she is one of their own confederates. Yet whereas some may object, that some of them that are cast fairly into the water, without holding up their feet with a string, do sink more than others, and some again do swim more than others (although none do sink quite away without any part appearing above water)

The reason of this difference is easie to conceive to men of knowledge; for, First; There is difference of constitution in peoples bodies; some are heavie of temper, and they sink most; some again are more light of temper, fuller of, vital spirits, and they sink not so much. Secondly, we must observe the Systole and Diastole of breathing; some happen to fall into the water when their bodies are full of breath, and they swim most; some happen to fall into the water when their breath is out of their bodies, before they can draw it up again, and they sink most. Some are kept long fasting in watching and torment, and then are cast into the water when their bowels and veins are empty of food and filled with Wind, and these swim more than those that are filled with nourishment; or perhaps they are kept fasting so long that they have scarce any life left, and then they happen to sink most, but if they do, it must not serve their turn, for the cruel Inquisitor will still torment them till he extort confession, if the party live long enough for his cruelty to take place. Some again are Women cast into the water, with their Coates tied close toward their feet, and Men with their apparrel on (and for this they pretend modesty) but who knoweth not that their apparrel will carry them above water for a time? Some again are Women, whose bodies are dilated with bearing of Children, and do always after remain spongiously hollow, more apt to swim than to sink, especially tied hands and feet together, to bring their bodies into a round and apt fashion to swim. They that are used to the Art of swimming in the water, might easily discover these to be but Delusions and Juglings, if they were not too credulous; and yet with these hath poor England been bewitched and deceived, as also with the former, of keeping the accused from sleep till they confess; and these delusions have been impiously acted here in England, of late in Essex, and Suffolk, by a wicked Inquisitor pretending authority for it, to the cutting off of fourteen innocent people at Chelmford Assizes, and about an hundred at Berry Assizes, whereof one was a Minister neer Fremingham, of about fourscore years age, wherein this Inquisitor hath laid such a president for the Popes Inquisition (if times of Popish Tyranny should again come in, from which God in his mercy defend us) as would not easily be removed, when although we have no Laws in England to try people upon Life and Death by any Inquisition, or Inquisitor, in that manner; yet it may then bee said, was it Law then; when the Law was in your hands, and is it not Law now? but if such times of tyrannous Inquisition come, do they that have had a hand in this president think they shall escape it, or their Posterity? There is already a president for killing of Ministers for Witches. Also some credulous people hearing of the Condemnation of those people, have published a Book, wherein they report such impossibilities to be done by them, as I hope no wise man will beleeve; wherein also Hoy, the Gaoler, is brought in for a Witness, a fellow, that is not fit to bear the Office of a Gaoler, nor any other Office in a Christian Common-wealth, who also wanted Vails, and thought the more Prisoners were executed, the more he should gain; and yet it is reported, his Testimony was taken as an Evidence against them, although his testimony was partly of impossibilities, partly meer prevarications and lyes, to the dis-honour of Gods Majesty, and the shedding of innocent bloud. But seeing then this miserable Massacre of people throughout the Christian World hath been but a trick of Antichrist, to blinde the World, that thereby he might the more easily and quietly destroy the Church under the name of Witches, Surely it good Christians have been destroyed in this impious way, then thousands of the Souls of such are now under the Altar, Revel. 6. 9, 10. crying, How long Lord, holy and true, will it be ere thou avenge our bloud upon them that dwell upon the earth? being some of them the very people that have been destroyed for the Word of God, and for the testimony of the truth; and therefore have been brought into these murderous Inquisitors hands; And although it may be said, These in England have not been slain for the testimony of the truth; yet I answer, The Church standeth for the testimony of the truth, and this persecution was invented against the Church, and so they as Members of the Church have been slain by the enemies invention; for had they been of that Popish crew, and fighters against the Church, those wrongful accusations had not been brought against them by them. But it may be said, Some of these were Scoulds and Brawlers, therefore their Souls are not under the Altar. I answer, yea, and many honest Livers that have been executed in that kinde lately, and in times past; but whatsoever they were, if they were unjustly slain, know, that if God would avenge the bloud of Cain, will he not avenge the bloud of these? Before the destruction of Germany, that Nation was so deluded by these Popish errours, that they put to death thousands in that kinde, of all sorts, and that Nation was so carried away with that darksome Idolatrous opinion of Witches power, that seldom came anything cross, but some were accused to have occasioned it as Witches, and at last God sent destroying Plagues among them, and their hearts were so hardened, that they digged the dead out of the Graves to cut off their Heads to stay the Plague; so blinde were they, and so given over, that rather than they would acknowledge Gods hand in all things, they would say, the dead in their Graves, by the Devils help, brought the plague; and some Physicians among them were so bold to affirm it for truth, who although they might be some way approved in Physick, yet besides their horrible Atheism, they shewed their silliness, and it may be said of them as of many ignorant Physicians, Inscitie pallium maleficium and incantatio; A Cloak for a Physicians ignorance, when he cannot finde the reason and the nature of the Disease, he saith, the Party is bewitched; this hath indeed been written of by some worthy Authors, but how, and in what manner? Senertus Lib. 4, de febribus, cap. 2, he being loath to defile his pen with such an impious opinion, saith, I had rather refer the Reader to the writing of another man, Hercul. Saxoniæ, Lib. de plica. cap. 11. than bring my self upon the Stage for breaching of such an opinion; where also you may read the words of Herc, Saxon, aforesaid, and thee shuffleth it off to Joh. Vefino Leopoliensi, as an opinion of his, and he like an Atheist did indeed own that opinion, That in Pelonia and Germany, Witches, after their execution and burial, did commonly send destroying pestilence; I think indeed the executing of so many innocent poor people did bring the Pestilence, and the Sword, and Famine, all against them, because they provoked God with their own inventions, tending not only to Idolatry, in imputing the Work of the Creator to a Creature, but also to the shedding of innocent bloud. Master Scot in his Discovery telleth us, That our English people in Ireland, whose posterity were lately barbarously cut off, were much given to this Idolatry in the Queens time, insomuch that there being a Disease amongst their Cattel that grew blinde, being a common Disease in that Country, they did commonly execute people for it, calling them eyebiting Witches; Great Britain hath been much infected with that Atheism, and many people both in England and Scotland have been by foolish false accusations put to death, for doing such things as are not in the power of men, or of Devils to do, but only of the Creator; And before these Wars began, what Atheistical reports were published of certain Lancashire people, that they could transform themselves into Grey-hounds, and into Men and Women again, and pull down Butter and other provision from the Air, (or from whence any crack-brained accuser would imagine?) When King Charls went last to Scotland before these Wars, as he came back again sayling over the River Humber, the Vessel in which his Plate was carried, was reported to be cast away, and then was that Atheism so great, even at the very Court of England, that they reported Witches had done it, instead of observing Gods supream Providence, (whereas Christ saith, A Sparrow shall not fall to the ground without Gods providence) since which we have had bloudy Wars, and where is the Court now? and now of late hath been in the year one thousand six hundred forty five, that great slaughter of Men and Women called Witches, at the Assizes at Eerry, and at Chelmoford, these poor accused people were watched day and night, and kept from sleep with much cruelty, till their Fancies being hurt, they would confess what their Inquisitors would have them, although it were a thing impossible, and flat contrary, to sense and Christian understanding to beleeve; (where, for the removing of Objections, it is to be noted, That a Fancy so hurt with watching, cannot afterward of a long time recant, or deny that which they have confessed, no more than a Hawk throughly tamed by watching can grow speedily wilde again, although you give them their full sleep; this manner of extorting confession, and seeming to convict them, being but a meer Jugling; Trick invented by the Pope, and their Trial in that kinde being Jugling Witchcraft it self, that may make the wisest man confess any thing though never so falfe) What troubles have followed this Slaughter, blinde men may see. A little before the Conquest of Scotland (as is reported upon good intelligence) the Presbytery of Scotland did, by their own pretended authority, take upon them to Summon, Convent, Censure, and Condemn people to cruel death for Witches and (as is credibly reported) they caused four thousand to be executed by Fire and Halter, and had as many in prison to be tried by them, when God sent his conquering Sword to suppress them, by occasion of which Wars there were many Ministers (whereof many were Presbyters) slain; What is become of their Presbyterian Authority now? Yet because there are some that slighting these observations will hardly be beaten from this conceit of Witches power, which they have so long beleeved, and will not yet think but that Witches have a familiar spirit, by whose help they kill, and act strange Wonders; tell me, where is a place in all the Scripture that saith so? shew me in all the Scriptures such a word, as Striges, lamiæ, Incubus, and Succubus, or any word of such signification or importance; what were Pharaoh his Magicians, but deluders of Pharaoh and the People? could they by the help of Satan do any thing truly? were they real Miracles? did not, their madnes come to light? 2 Tim. 3. 9. what spirit had the Maid that followed Paul? Act. 16. 16. which is said to have the spirit of Python, was it more than a cousening spirit of Divination, for gain? yet still you will say, the word Python hath been interpreted by many, one that had a familiar spirit; imagine they had a familiar spirit (although it is but a weak Argument to ground an opinion upon the bare signification of a word (except you will have it a seducing lying spirit, such a one as was in Ahabs Prophets) yet I say, answer me these Four Questions. First, Tell we where a Witch did, or could kill a man in Scripture? What did Saul go to the Pythonist of Endor for? was it that she might help him kill the Philistians, or meerly for Augury or Divination? what did Pharaoh call his Witches the Magicians before him for? was it to kill any Man or Beast by their cunning? or meerly to work lying Wonders, and dissemble the Miracles that God wrought by Moses? so that they might withstand Mofes, and the truth, and blinde Pharaohs eyes, because God would harden his heart; tell me where you finde in all the Scriptures, that a Witch did, or could kill a man by Witchcraft; shew me in all the Law of Moses concerning the condemning of men or women for Murther, that a Murtherer was called a Witch, or a Witch a Murtherer, Deut. 19. and other places of Scripture; are there not several Rules set down for the trying of Murther? shew me one that intimateth the Witching of Men or Cattel to death? Secondly, Shew me in all the Scriptures where Witches are spoken of, that a Witch was a secret person, or unknown to the World, that should need to be tried by blinde circumstances, and presumptions, and suspicions, or by privie Marks, or by Teats, or Biggs, by sinking or swimming, or by confessions? were not Pharaohs Witches called Prastigiatores and magi, openly known? did not Pharaoh call them together without privie search, or inquiry? did not Saul banish all the Witches as people openly known, and professing the Art of Augury, and their several cousening practices? when Saul inquired for a Witch, did not his servants presently tell him there was one at Endor, was she not known without privie search, or prime marks? did not the Maid in the Acts, that was said to have the spirit of Python, or to be a Pythonift, follow Paul, crying openly? did not Simon Magus act his Delusions openly, to seduce the people? as likewise Elimas the Sorcerer? were not the Witchcrafts of Jezabel known to be her delusions that she wrought by the Priests of Baal, to seduce the people? were not the Witchcrafts of Manasses open actions, that made Juda and Jerusalem to go astray? where then do we read of a Witch by suspicion, or to be tried by presumptions, or suspicions, or privie marks, or other signs that are mans invention? whence came this darkness and blinde errour, but from the Pope, that grand Witch that hath bewitched all Nations? we search for Witchcrafts and abominations in a poor womans wooden dish, and Christ telleth us, they are all in a cup of Gold, in the hand of the great Whore, Revel. 17. 4. Thirdly, Shew me in all the

Scriptures where Witchcraft went without Idolatry, Ifa. 19. 3. and had not a necessary dependance on Idolatry, Nahum 3. 4. Look again, Deut. 18. 10, 11. where all sorts of Witches are spoken of, why were they to be cut off and destroyed? the reason is immediatly given, vers. 14. because they defiled the Nations, in seducing them unto Spiritual Whoredom, and the Nations were destroyed for seeking, and making inquiry after then Divinations, or South-sayings, on Oracles, whereas inquiries ought to be to Gods Prophets, vers. 15. Was not this Sauls Idolatry, when he sought to the Witch of Endor? I Chro. 10. 13, 14. was not this the sin of Manasses, where he is blamed for using Witchcrafts, when he made Juda and Jerusalem go astray to Idols? 2 Chron. 83. 9. were not the Witchcrafts and Whoredoms of Jesabel let down as two inseparable companions, her Witchcraft being the upholding of the Idol Priests of Baal, that by Witchcraft seduced the people to Idolatry? were not Pharaohs Magicians seducers of Pharaoh, and the people, from God? was not Simon Magus the like? but alas, how, and where have those poor souls that are commonly hanged for Witches seduced the people to Idolatry? who hath been led after them for Divinations, and Southsayings? many indeed have been led after Southsayers, but they are termed good Witches, and whereas they as Witches ought to dye, many have been put to death by their devillish false accusations, and if the Witch of Endor were now living amongst us, we should call her a good Witch, so blinde are the times. Fourthly, Shew me in all the Law of God against Adulterous uncleaneness (where Moses writeth of several kindes of uncleaneness, as man with man, man with beast, woman with beast, and many more) the least intimation of uncleanness, by Incubus, or Succubus; what, did Moses forget this? Yet because this opinion hath been so upheld by reports and imaginations, and by the extorted confession of people that have been condemned in that kinde, and sometime by the voluntary confession of despairing melancholly people that have been troubled in minde, and wish rather to dye than to live, although Volentimori, non est adhibendat fides; Yet I intreat you to run over these several places of Scripture with me a little, and see how this opinion of Witches power agreeth with the Scriptures, yea how flat contrary it is to Gods Word, and the grounds of our Christian faith. Yet first, because some men will not understand the Scriptures in any other sense than as their own Expositors have done, be it right or wrong; therefore. I refer them that will seek farther than the Scriptures, to the words of a general Counsel, which Mr. Scat in his Discovery hath alleged as followeth, Concil. Acqui, in decret. 26. the words of the Council. It may not be omitted, that certain wicked Women following Satans provocations, being seduced by the illusion of the Devil, beleeve, and profess that in the night time they ride abroad with Diana the Goddess of the Pagans, or else with Herodias, with an innumerable multitude, upon certain Beasts, and pass over many Countries and Nations in the silence of the night, and do whatsoever these Ladies or Fairies command, and c. let all Ministers therefore in their several Cures preach to Gods people so, as they may know all those things to be false, and whosoever beleeveth that any Creature can be made by them, or changed into better or worse, or be any way transformed into any other kinde, or likeness, by any but by the Creator himself, is assuredly an Infidel, and worse than a Pagan. So much for the words of the Council. Yet here is to be noted, that this great general Council, that thought these people beleeved, and confessed such things to be true in their apprehension, did not then know the inhuman cruelty that was used upon those people by the cruel Inquisitors to compel, and extort confession for their own gain, they being maintained by the spoyl of such people being condemned. Now for the Scriptures, do but mark how those that maintain, and report the power of Witches, have equalled their supernatural power, with the Miracles of the Prophets, of Christ, and his Apostles; it was the Miracle of Miracles, that the Virgin Mary conceived with childe without a man; they say, a Witch may do the same by Incubus, as Bodin, and other Popish Writers affirm, and that such a childe will naturally become a Witch, such a one they say Merlin was; no, but you say these were Atheists, we beleeve not so; But some will say, the Devil can condense a body,

III

and lye carnally with a woman in the shape of a man, but not beget; yet it was a Miracle that Angels appeared to Abraham in the shape of men, Gen. 18. 2. yet they will say no, but we beleeve the Devil may assume and raise a dead body for a time, and so appear to a woman, and lye with her; and yet it was a Miracle at the suffering of Christ upon the Cross, that dead bodies were raised for a time, and appeared to many, Matth. 27. 52. yet a poor Wench was executed at the Assizes at Chelmsford, who was compelled by the Inquisitor (by keeping her from sleep and with promises and threatnings) to confess that she was married to the Devil, and that he lay with her six times in a mans shape; no, but yet some will say, the Devil can take upon him an apparent Body, and so may talk with a woman, and seem to lye with her in shape of a man, and so she shall be hanged for things seeming so; yet it was a Miracle that Moses and Elias appeared to the Apoftles in a Vision, Matth. 17. 3. Further, Christ saith, A Spiris hath not flesh and bones, Lake 24. 39. and yet some say, the Devil can condense a body, some say he can assume a body, some say he can have an apparent body; thus do they make the Word of God of no validity by their groundless traditions; for if the Devil can have so much as an apparent body, what validity was in the words of Christ, to take away the doubt of the Disciples, when they supposed they saw a Spirit? Where also is that foolish Doctrin of Imps, sucking of men and women-Witches become? Are those Imps bodies or spirits? if bodies, then who made them? Without God was nothing made, Joh. 1. 3. if spirits, then spirits can have bodily shape, and flesh, and bones; and thus you make the words of Christ of none effect by your traditions. Christ dispersed Devils to enter into the Herd of Swine, and they went, Mark 5. 12. they say a Witch can do more; she can send the Devil into men and women, and children, and cartel, to kill them, and to witch them to death. God said to Satan, All that Job hath is in thine hand, Job 1. 12. and Job himself, all but his life, Job 2. 6. they say, God permitteth a Witch to do more, to send Satan to destroy a mans goods, and cattel, and children, and life and all; thus they deliver for Doctrin the traditions of men. Job said, The

Lord giveth, and the Lord taketh away, blessed be the name of the Lord, and acknowledged Gods hand in all things, neither tempted he God foolishly; But if one should be so afflicted now adays, instead of acknowledging Gods sovereign hand, all the poor Wives and Widows in a Country must be called Coram nobis, as being accused to have done it. Christ saith, Revel. I. 18. I have the keys of Hell and Death, but they say, God giveth the keys of Death likewise sometimes to an old Witch (man or woman) and permits them to witch men to death; Christ saith, A Sparrow falleth not to the ground without Gods providence, Matth. 10 29. but they say, God layeth his providence sometimes at the feet of an old Witch, and permitteth her to send the Devil to destroy men and cattel; some will say, A Witch cannot hurt a godly man, but only a wicked man, and yet God saith, he is the Author of all affliction that cometh to the wicked, Levit. 26. from the fourteenth verse to the thirty fourth. Also the Scripture saith, The Lord killeth and maketh alive, I Sam. 2. 6. maketh poor, and maketh rich; and in Deut. 32. 39 There is no God with me, I kill and give life, I wound and make whole; but they say, God permitteth an old Witch to send the Devil to kill, and make poor, and wound, and a good Witch can heal again by unwitching. God did shut up every wombe of the House of Abimelech, that they bare no children, Gen. 20. 18. they say a Witch can do the same (God permits it) and make men and women barren. Christ gave his Disciples power over Devils, to cast them out, Luke 9. I. they say, a Witch can send a Devil into men and cattel to afflict them, and a good Witch can cast them out by unwitching, notwithstanding, Christ, saith, Matth. 12. 25. Every kingdom divided against it self is brought to desolation; yet they say, that is done by consent of the Devil, when a good Witch unwitcheth a man; thus do they make the words of Christ of none effect by their traditions. Christ came and appeared unto his Disciples, and vanished away again invisible, Luke 24. 31. they say, a Witch can go invisible by the help of the Devil, especially if one of the Ladies of the Fairies will but lend her Giges invisible ring. Christ was lifted up into the Air, and taken up out of their sight, Acts I.

9. and Bodinus and other Popish Writers affirm, that a Witch can be lifted away in the Air by drinking the broth of a sodden Infant; but poor Germany, that beleeved these Doctrins, and in that confidence executed many people for Witches, was compelled afterward to boyl their children to quell their hunger, and found by sad experience that there was no such vertue in that woful Liquor. God said to Moses, Go up into the mountain and dye, Deut. 32. 49, 50. and he did so, Chap. 34. vers. 5. they say a Witch can do so at the word of the Devil, and dye when she lift, to escape hanging; and what is a more common report when a poor woman is laid in prison, and there dyeth by grief and hard usage, than to report, the Devil promised her the should not be hanged, and was as good as his word, for she dyed in prison before the day of Execution came; thus do they make the Devil able to determine, and limit the life of Man, as God did the life of Moses. It is said in Isa. 41. 23. Shew what is to come after, that we may know yee are gods; They say, a Witch can truly foretel things to come by her spirit of Divination (which they call a Familiar) and can by the same familiar tell what is done in another Town, or House, or Country, and can tell a man where are his Goods that are lost, as well as Samuel could tell Saul of his Fathers Asses when they were lost, and such they call good Witches. Also in the same Verse, Esa. 41. 23. it followeth in the end of the verse, do good, or do evil, that we may be dismsayed, and behold it together; these words have relation to the former words, That we may know that ye are gods; that is, shew what is to come hereafter, or do good, or do evil, that we may know ye are gods, and be dismayed at your doings (even as when God sendeth the evil of punishment or affliction upon a people, then they are dismayed at the sight and apprehension of it,) as in Job 40. 11. And here when we read that God claimeth the doing thereof as his own Prerogative, inferring as much as to say, They are gods that can do this, I think that after the reading of this verse in Isaiah, and Job, no man should be so grosly Idolatrous still, as to ascribe to a Witch the sending of any affliction; those words also, Do good, or do evil, (the whole verse having relation

to the seventh verse) were spoken to the Idol Priests of the Heathen, who were the Witches mentioned in the Scriptures, and had as great a share in the Devil, as any Witch can have, and yet God challengeth them to do either good or evil; and yet when any evil of affliction cometh upon Men or Beast, these Idolaters will still ascribe it to a Witch, saying still, God permits it. God sent an evil spirit upon Saul to vexe him, I Sam. 16. 14. they say a Witch can send an evil spirit upon men or women to vex or torment them; Elisha cursed two and forty children in the name of the Lord, and they were destroyed of Bears, 2 King. 2. 24. they say a Witch can curse men and women in the name of the Devil, and Death or some other Evil shall betide them. Pharaohs Magicians, though they were themselves Witches, yet when they saw Lice creeping upon Men and Beast, they acknowledged the finger of God. They, if they see a man smitten with a lousie disease as Herod was, say presently he is bewitched. It was a great Miracle that Christ made the Wind and the Sea obey him, Mark 4. 41. they say Witches can do the same, and raise Winds and Tempests, and make it calm at their pleasure. Was not this one accusation that was brought against Mr. Lewis a Minister executed at Berry Assizes, that he had raised a Tempest, and cast away two Ships at sea by Witchcraft? Christ by his Almighty power walked upon the waters, Mat. 14. 25. they say, cast a Witch into the waters and she will not sink; and what hath been more reported and beleeved than this Jugling delusion before spoken of? God claimeth it as his own Prerogative to send Lightnings and Thunders, Job 38. 25, 35. but they say, when it Thundereth or Lighteneth, that Witches do sometimes cause it, especially if it be at an Assize time, when many Witches are condemned; and what hath been a more common report than this, when God hath sent thundring voyces from Heaven at an Assize time among the people, to warn them, instead of discerning that God was angry, they say, the Witches and the Devil was angry, and have caused that thundet? God teacheth us in Levit. 26. that he himself sendeth Barrenness, and Famine, Sword, and Pestilence, and all Diseases, and all Adversities, as the punishment of Sin, but which of these have not been ascribed to Witches? and if the several accusations of people that have been condemned for Witches, but only here in England, within the memory of man were Registred, we might read such a hotch potch of impossibilities, as he that beleeveth that they have been justly put to death, must not beleeve the Scriptures, nor ascribe any thing to Gods mighty Providence, but he may also ascribe it to the will and pleasure of a Witch; when Christ did by the Spirit of God cast out Devils, and the Pharisees ascribed that work to Beelzebub, Christ chargeth them with the sin against the Holy Ghost, Matth. 12. 28, 31. but alas, how common a thing is it to ascribe to the Devil and Witches, the works that God telleth us in the holy Scriptures are his own Works, and cannot be done by any other power but by the Spirit of God? me thinks this should scare all obstinate Witchmongers. I heard a Suffolk Minister (whose habit and garb might seem to claim the title of Rabbi, Rabbi) affirm, that one of the poor women that was hanged for a Witch at Berry Assizes, in the year 1645. did send her Imps into the Army, to kill the Parliaments Souldiers, and another sent her Imps into the Army to kill the Kings Souldiers, and another caused a mans crop of Corn to fail, and caused that Corn which he had to be blasted, and tipt, or crockt, and this Minister did verily affirm that those things were true, for the Witches (said he) confessed those things; but when I came to argue with him, and to tell him that these things in the Scripture-sense were Gods Prerogatives, he could answer nothing, he was not so well skilled in the Scriptures; but he replied, Thou shalt not suffer a Witch to live. I demanded of him, what was the signification of the Hebrew text, or of the Latine translation, and what was meant by a Witch in that place, he could not tell; thus hath the salt of the earth lost its favour; and whereas those should season people with wholsome Doctrin, some teach Doctrins of Devils, and the inventions of Antichrist, to defile the Nations. And people are now so infected with this damnable Heresie, of ascribing to the power of Witches, that seldom hath a man the hand of God against him in his estate, or health of body, or any way, but presently he cryeth out of some poor innocent Neighbour, that he, or she hath bewitched him; for saith he, such an old man or woman came lately to my door, and desired some relief, and I denied it, and God forgive me, my heart did rise against her at that time, my mind gave me she looked like a Witch, and presently my Child, my Wife, my Self, my Horse, my Cow, my Sheep, my Sow, my Hogge, my Dogge, my Cat, or somewhat was thus and thus handled, in such a strange manner, as I dare swear she is a Witch, or else how should those things be, or come to pass? seldom goeth any man or woman to a Physician for cure of any Disease, but one question they ask the the Physician is, Sir, do you not think this Party is in ill handling, or under an ill tongue? or more plainly, Sir, do you not think the party is bewitched? and to this many an ignorant Physician will answer, Yes verily; the reason is, Ignorantiæ pallium maleficium and incantatio, a cloak for a Physicians ignorance, when he cannot finde the nature of the Disease, he saith, the Party is bewitched. But for all such as go on to defile the people with these Doctrins, that not only have no grounds in the Scriptures, but are flat contrary to the light of the Scriptures. I demand of them, at whose hands will Christ require at the latter day, not only the bloud of the innocent, but also the Souls of such as have perished by the practice of these Atheistical and bloud-guilty ways? which are in every point so absurd and phantastical, that if many Ministers can say they never did teach any such Doctrin to the people, yet are they guilty, in that they have not preached against these devillish Doctrins, which do make against the true worship of God, and against the life of charity toward our Neighbour, and toward the poor and widows, and lame and aged people. Many Objections and evasions are daily brought against this my Discourse, which though they are weak and frivolous, yet would fill whole Volumes if I would stand to answer them. I The common evasion of every one when they can prove nothing, nor answer, but are fully convinced of their errours by the Scriptures, is, Say no more, we acknowledge that a Witch can do no more than God permits her, or permits him to do, but what God permits, that a Witch can do; this is just as when God and his Prophets taught the people early and late, that they should not ascribe any power to Idols, as if the people had answered the Prophets, Say no more, we know these Idols can do no more than God permits them to do, but if God permit them to save, or destroy, they can do it. So when God claimeth it as his own Prerogative, to kill and make alive, make rich and make poor, wound and heal, (and many other things, as I have already proved by Scripture) and will not have his Prerogative ascribed to any Creature, yet still ye say, the Lord permits it, whereas yet yee have no more ground or warrant in the Scripture, that God permits any such power to Witches, than the Heathen had to say, the most high God permitted their Idols also to be gods, and to have power to kill, or to save alive. Further, Ye say, God permits one man to murther another, yet for this the murtherer ought to be slain; that is true indeed, but for that yee have Scripture, where yee read in the Law, of Murther, how it was to be judged, that is, if one man did wilfully smite another with his hand, or any other material instrument, that he dyed, it was murther, Numb. 35. 16. and so forward, but where do you read that God permits any such thing to come to pass by a Witch, or that any man can kill another by Witchcraft, or without a material Instrument? and when it is proved by many places of Scripture, that many such things as yee ascribe to Witches are Gods Prerogative, yet still yee cry, God permits it. 2 Another Objection is this, It is certain that there are some people in Germany, and Polonia, that do commonly sell Winds by the Devils help to Sea-men, to carry their ships whither they intend; therefore a Witch can make a League with the Devil, and by his help can raise Winds. To this I answer, I do not deny but these are Witches, because they use Impostures to deceive the world, and seduce them to that damnable Idolatry of ascribing to the Devil and Witches, and seeking to them for that which belongeth to God alone to give, namely Winds for their Journey; but that they do such things really without delusion is false, which I will first prove by Scripture, and then shew you the delusion; for Scripture, first I prove, if they can by the Devils raise Winds, then they can also send fair weather, for the North-wind driveth away rain, as. Job 37. 22. fair weather cometh out of the North, and Job. 38. 24. God speaking of his own mighty work saith, By what way is the light parted, which scattereth the East wind upon the earth? and Job. I. 3. Without God was nothing made, who then maketh these winds? Psal. 148. 8. the Winds fulfill the Word of God, or blow at Gods decree. Also Solomon reckoneth the Winds among such things as keep a natural course, and describeth the natural course thereof, Eccles. I. 6. Also things miraculous can be done by God only, but that was one of the Miracles by which Christ shewed himself to be God, he made the winds and the sea obey him, Mark 4. 41. Also it is an absurdity in Philosophy, to say that a Witch, or the Devil, can cause Winds, for Winds are exhalations drawn from the Earth, by the influence of the Sun and the Stars, and driven back by the coldness of the middle region of the Air, which causeth their several motions, and therefore he that saith a Witch or a Devil can cause Winds, must ascribe also to them that they can rule the Stars, and dispose the quality of the middle Region, by which it must follow that they can send what weather they list, and so by consequence cause the earth to bring forth, or to be barren, which were the height of Idolatry to beleeve. And now to come to the imposture it self, wherewith the foresaid Impostors do deceive fools, making them beleeve they sell them Winds for their Journy. The poor Mariner who desireth to hasten his Journey homewards (but withall considereth not that all men must wait upon Providence) saith, I would give five pounds the Winds would rise, or that they would turn fit for our Journey; and being among strangers he is presently over-heard by some of the Factors of those Impostors, who presently take occasion to tell him, that they will undertake for half the money, to carry him to one that shall help him to a Wind according to his minde, then by degrees they draw him on till they bring him into the company of more of their Confederates, who do so cunningly combine to obscure his intellect by discourse, that at the last they lead him (like poor Saul, when the

Spirit of God had forsaken him) to seek to a Witch, then do they lead him to the Impostor, who being some skilful Aftrologian in those Countries, can give a neer guess by the Stars, when such a Wind will arise, and accordingly prefixeth a day, saying, a week hence, or two days bence, or sometimes a fortnight hence you shall have a Wind, in which promise it often happeneth that the Impostor himself is deceived, when his Prognosticks fail him; and then they prefixe another day, and do strongly perswade the silly man to stay till then, whereas they know till the Winds rise he cannot but stay, and I my self have talked with Seamen, who confess that sometimes they have been driven to stay a week, sometimes longer, after the day prefixed, and after they parted with then; money; but if it happeneth that fome man after he hath laid out his money upon those Impostors, hath speedily a Wind for his Journey; then he rejoyceth, and then the Impostors are credited; then he receiveth from the Impostor a bottom of Thread, which the Impostor Saith he had from such an old Woman (because he will not seem to be the Witch himself) and this Thread is to be carried by the Mariner, or by the Merchant, into the Ship, and he must by degrees continually unwinde the bottom of Thread, so long as he would have that Wind blow; but if all things happen well, then it is concluded, surely it is by vertue of the Thread ; but if Winds prove by the way cross, then it is the fault of him that unwindeth the bottome too fast, or too slow, or with the wrong hand ; and thus are poor Idolatrous fools cheated by them that make a rich trade of their Imposture. I deny not but this delusion is variously acted in several Countries, and some Travellours report some one way, and some another way of the manner, and carriage of the Imposture ; but he that beleeveth that it is really done, and not a deceiving impofture, is an Idolater, and as bad as an Infidel, and for such Mariners as will buy Winds in that manner, the Mariness of Tarshish shall rise up in judgement against them, who when they saw the Wind rise, and the Sea rempestuous, and against their Voyage, they sought for whose sin that evil was come upon them, Jonah I. 7. those poor Heathen knew that Winds and Tempests came not from a Witch, but from the hand of God. To conclude, stories reported by Travellours prove nothing, neither are they lawful Objections, and when we hear such a thing reported contrary to the Scriptures, and to human capacity, it must needs follow that it is a deluding imposture, although the story be true from him that reporteth it; and some Travellours that report this thing, yet are perswaded in themselves that it is but deceit. And whereas some would confirm this Objection by Scripture, because it is said, Job. I. 19. after God had said to Satan, All that Job hath is in thy power, there came a strong Wind from the Wilderness, and smote the house that it fell upon the young men that they dyed. Hence they argue, that the Devil raised that wind; but this is a false conclusion, for then they may as well argue that the Devil sent the fire from Heaven, as in vers, 16. which is yet called the fire of God; and Job himself ascribed all to God only, vers. 21. Secondly, If the Devil had by Gods peculiar dispensation raised that Wind, God permitting him to afflict Job, yet it doth not follow that he can do it at the command of a Witch. Thirdly, Some to prove the power of Witches to afflict men, and women, and cattel, and to bring to pass strange things, do alledge Job 2. 7. yet there is not a Witch mentioned in all the History of Job, but how absurdly they do argue let wise men judge; because God sent Satan to afflict Job, therefore a Witch can send him to afflict man. God permitteth it, say they, by which Argument they still labour to maintain that God lendeth his Prerogatives to a Witch. What though God hath power over Satan, to command him to execute his Will, to torment and afflict the wicked for punishment, to afflict the righteous sometime for trial? doth it therefore follow that a Witch can do it, because God did it? and where do we read in Scripture that God permits it? and if God should permit it, where do we read that a Witch hath any suchpower or command over the Devil, or any such league or covenant with the Devil? or that God permits the Devil to be at the command of a Witch? Fourthly, Some will allege the Witch of Endor, and yet we never read that the Witch of Endor could hurt, or send the Devil to hurt any man or woman, or childe, or cattel, or raise Winds, or the like; neither did Saul go to her to desire her to kill the Philistines, but he went for Divinations, to know what should become of the Battel the next day. And what Objections soever any man shall bring from the Witch of Endor, they themselves may answer, if they read but the Seventh description of a Witch, in the first Book of this Treatise, and he that was bewitched by the Witch of Endor was Saul, and such as sought to her as Saul did, because they were deluded by her. Fifthly, Some will allege, and object, That the Serpent tempted Eve, and from thence they will argue, that the Devil can assume the bodies of Creatures, and appear in bodily shape, and make a league with a Witch, and execute her will to kill and afflict people and cattel; but this is a poor consequence, that because he can tempt, therefore he can kill at the command of a Witch; and whereas they would prove from hence, that the Devil can assume a bodily shape, and appear to a Witch, if they bring that Argument from the literal sence of the History, they must search narrowly to prove the Devil was in the Serpent; for it is said, The Serpent was more subtile than any beast of the field, inferring that the Serpent did tempt by its own natural subtilty, or else why was that expression of the subtilty thereof used by Moses? and hence they must conclude, that it was the Serpent, and not the Devil, which tempted Eve, which were an absurd conclusion; and yet if they run upon the letter of the Story, they cannot deny that conclusion to follow, for there is not any mention of the Devil in all the History; but if they could prove thence that the Devil did assume the body of the Serpent, it maketh nothing to the purpose, to prove Witches power to kill, for the Devil did only beguile Eve, and not kill her. And although it hath been a common exposition of that place, that the Devil did enter into the body of the Serpent, and so appeared unto Eve in a bodily shape, and talked with her, and tempted her to eat the forbidden Fruit, yet if this exposition be well and wisely considered, it is most gross and erroneous ; for First, here ariseth an absurdity, according to their own fond tenents, for then they must conclude that Eve was a Witch, for say they, whosoever hath had any familiar discourse with the Devil is in some degree a

Witch, and ought not to be trusted, although the hath made no compact with the Devil, and I have known some hanged in my time for that confession, although they did absolutely deny that ever they made compact with him, or did any murther by him ; but yet to speak the truth, if it were so, that any man or woman could have familiar discourfe with the-Devil, this maketh not a Witch, for Christ himself was assaulted by the Devil, and answered his tentations by Scriptum est, Matth. 4. yea, I may further say, if any man could enter into an explicite covenant with the Devil to kill by his help, this indeed would make him a Murtherer, but not a Witch in the Scripture sense, although indeed no man can prove by Scripture any such compact at all, or if there could be such a compact made with the Devil, yet that God would ever permit the Devil to perform his covenant with a man, to kill or hurt at his command, cannot be proved. So much by the way. Secondly, There ariseth another absurdity directly from that exposition, that the Devil did enter into the body of the Serpent, and so tempted Eve, for thence it must needs follow, that the Devil can open the mouth of a Serpent, and cause it to speak, and talk, and so that the Devil should have power to work a Miracle, equal with that great Miracle that was wrought by the mighty power of God, when he opened the mouth of Balaams Asse, and caused him to speak to Balaam, which thing were most outragious Blasphemy to affirm; we must needs conclude then, that it was neither the Serpent that by its own natural subtilty tempted Eve, as the letter of the Story importeth, nor the Devil abusing the body of the Serpent; But whereas Moses was here to teach the people a great mystical Doctrin concerning the fall of Mankind by sin, unto which sin man was drawn by the temptations and allurements of the Devil; Moses knowing that the capacity of weak people is naturally estranged from Spiritual matters, and if he should have taught in plain terms that the Devil tempted man to fall, they would not have understood his Doctrin, because they Knew not what the Devil was, therefore he, by the Spirit of God guiding him, taught the people, in a Parabolical way, in which Parable when he speaketh of the Serpent, and of his subtilty, he expresseth the subtilty and malice of the Devil that tempted Eve, and all Mankind to disobedience against God, and this Parable he followeth Allegorically, when he saith, The Lord said unto the Serpent, upon thy belly shalt thou go, and dust shalt thou eat all the days of thy life; whereas if we deny this to be a Parable, we must hold that the Serpent before that time had leggs, and did not creep upon his belly, and also that the Serpent sinned, and is punished for sin; and yet if the Devil had power to abuse the body of the Serpent, the Serpent was compelled to do that which they say he did; but for those that will take the Scriptures every where in a literal sence, they must also hold that the Trees of the Feild did speak, where it is said in a Parable, The trees said to the Olive-tree, be thou King over us, Judg. 9. 8. But yet if they will not be beaten off from this, that the Devil can assume a bodily shape, it maketh nothing to prove that Witches are such people as can kill by Witchcraft, or send the Devil to kill, for there is no such expression of a Witch in all the Scriptures, but only that a Witch is such a one as laboureth by Diabolical craft to seduce the people from God, and his Truth, to Idolatry, and beleeving of lyes. Sixthly, Some will object, and say, It is manifest that the Devil can help a Witch to fly in the Air, and be transported whither she listeth, or else how had the Devil power to carry Christ, and set him upon the pinacle of the Temple? Matth. 4. and Luke 4. I answer, This indeed seemeth to be a strong Argument, if we take the Scriptures at the second hand, as they are translated unto us in the English, but if we search the original meaning of the Greek text (as it was written by the Spirit of God) we shall finde there is no strength at all in that Argument, for St. Luke, 4. 5. saith only, [Greek omitted], quem subduxisset eum, Or subducens eum, and in the ninth verse is the same sense, and so translated by Tremellius and Beza, and no otherwise to be understood, but that he was led by the Devil from place to place to be tempted (not that the Devil had power to lead him against his will) but being full of the Holy Ghost, did by his own Divine counsel yeeld so farre to the Devil, as to be led into temptation, that so he might overcome temptation; and whereas St. Matthew useth another phrase, [Greek omitted], assumpsit eum Diabolus, vers. 5. 8. this soundeth indeed (especially in some of our English translations) as if the Devil had transported him in the Air from place to place, but it was nothing so; if we compare Matthew and Luke together, and this phrase used by Matthew, saith Trernellius, is by a Metalepsis, so that it is plain this Objection is of no force, for Christ walked up to the Mountain, and likewise walked up the stayers of the Temple, and leaned upon, and looked over the Battlements of the Temple, which went round about the Temple to keep men from falling, of which we read, saith Beza, Deut. 22. 8. which we falsly translate, Pinacles, [Greek omitted], and hee set him against the Battlements of the Temple. Seventhly, Another Objection ariseth from this Discourse, and that is this; It seemeth the Devil can some way talk and discourse with a Witch, and therefore can make a League and Covenant with her: for he talked and discoursed with Christ himself, how much more easily can he talk with a sinfull man or woman? I answer, In the same manner that he talked with Christ, he talketh with every man and woman; he saith to a Thief, Steal; to a Cut-purse, Cut a Purse; to a Drunkard, Drink off your liquor; to a Murtherer, Kill such a man, and these obey him; he saith to a righteous man, Steal, and he answereth, It is written thou shalt not steal; the Devil saith again, Go and lye with such a Whore; he answereth, It is written, thou shalt not commit Adultery, and so likewise for all the Commandements; neither is it to be understood otherwise of the temptations wherewith Christ was tempted; as if the Devil could utter a human voyce without a tongue, or any organ of speaking, that were an absurdity in Philosophy, for Naturænihil fecit frustra; and this were superfluous in Nature for a man to have a Tongue, and other Organs of speaking, if a verbal speaking could be made without them; and whereas it is written, that the Devil said unto Christ this and that, it was only a mental discourse between Christ and the Devil, and is expressed in Scripture, according to Human capacity by a prosapopoia, a Figure very frequent in Scripture, as in Psal.98.8. Micha 6.12. there the Scripture by this

Figure bringeth in Hills and Flouds acting as a man; and so in Mat.4.Luke 4. the Devil tempting of Christ is introduced in the story, as speaking like a man, this is used sometimes in Parables, as in Job, from the seventh verse of the first Chapter to the twelfth, also Chap. 2. the six first verses; and in Gen. 3. 1. I King. 22. 21. in these and many places by this Figure, speaking and discoursing verbally, and Human action is ascribed to such as it doth not properly belong; so that it appeareth to those that rightly understand, that this objection also is of no force; but yet still for those that are obstinate, I say, let them prove a League or Covenant by the Scriptures, between the Devil and a Witch, or that the Devil hath power, or permission to perform such a Covenant if made. Eighthly, Some again will object and say, If Witches can not kill, and do many strange things by Witchcraft, why have many confessed that they have done such Murthers, and other strange matters, where of they have been accused? To this I answer, If Adam and Eve in their innocency were so easily overcome, and tempted to sin, how much more may poor Creatures now after the Fall, by perswasions, promises, and threatnings, by keeping from sleep, and continual torture, be brought to confess that which is false and impossible, and contrary to the faith of a Christian to beleeve? Some indeed have in a melancholly distraction of minde confessed voluntarily, yea and accused themselves to bee Witches, that could do, and had done such strange things, and wonders by the help of the Devil; but mark well their distemper, and you shall finde that they are deeply gone by infirmity of body affecting the minde, whereby they conceit such things as never were, or can be, as is often proved by experience among Physicians, many of those dying in a very short time, (although they be not put to death) except they be cured by the Physician; and truly if such Doctrins had not been taught to such people formerly, their melancholly distempers had not had any such objects to work upon, but who shall at last answer for their confession, but they that have infected the mindes of common people with such devillish doctrins, whereby some are instigated to accuse their poor Neighbours of impossibilities contrary to the Scriptures, and some drawn to confess lyes, and impossibilities contrary to Christian light? And indeed vain and fickle are the mindes of such disputants, who do first of all father their vain opinions upon the Scriptures, pretending that they are undoubted truths grounded upon the Scriptures, saying, Thou shalt not suffer a Witch to live; but being shewed their errours, how they wrest the Scriptures, will rather forsake the Scriptures, which are the rule of righteousness, then forsake their Opinions, and will beleeve confession against the Scriptures. Some men will yet yeeld thus farre, that these Confessions of poor accused people do many times extend to impossibilities, and that they verily beleeve that the Devil deludeth these people, making them beleeve that he bringeth to pass such things as they require him to do, which yet would come to pass by Divine providence. Some again do so Idolize the Devil, as that they affirm that these things are real, and do withall cry out, Great is the power of the Devil; and yet for any of these Opinions can produce no Scriptures to prove them, but only Confessions; and although those Confessions are sometimes extorted, sometimes voluntary in poor melancholy, or distracted people; sometimes in wicked people, who delight to make the world wonder at lyes, or impossibilities, though it be to their own confusion (they being given over by God, and so the Devil seeing his opportunity, instigateth them to be his Instruments to uphold all lying Diabolical Doctrins, so that no true beleeving Christian but may discern that all R these Confessions are from the Devil, the Father of lyes) yet I say, Suppose with these Confession-mongers, that these Confessors are deluded by Satan, to think they do such things by the help of the Devil, yet where do we read in Scripture that such are Witches who are deluded by Satan, or that such should be slain, or put to death? we read indeed, that Witches were all sorts of deluding false Prophets, but not such as were deluded by Satan. Secondly, If you will still affirm, that their Confessions are real truths, and not delusions, but that they do indeed bid the Devil do such things, which (as yee say) he doth; yet how can yee prove it by Scripture? where is any such description of a Witch in the Scripture? but surely it is most horrible devillish forsaking of the Scriptures, to beleeve that there is any truth at all in these Confessions, and such people as are thus seduced by Satan to lying Confession, ought rather to be taught better knowledge, than to be slain in their ignorance, and perish altogether for lack of knowledge; but it is, and hath been the manner of these latter Ages, for a Minister to go to such, and instead of instructing them, whereby they might become instruments of saving their souls, they urge them to lying Confessions, and so do as much as they can to send the spirit of errour into them to their confusion, yea and for the most part, these men who uphold their errours by the Confessions of these poor accused people, do altogether mis-interpret their Confessions for the upholding of such lyes, for the broaching whereof they have formerly mis-interpreted and belyed the Scriptures; for let but any man that is wise, and free from prejudice, go and hear but the Confessions which are so commonly alleged, and he may see with what catching, and cavelling, what thwarting and lying, what flat and plain Knavery these Confessions are wrung from poor innocent people, and what monstrous additions and multiplications are afterward invented to make the matter seem true, which yet is most damnably false, and flat against Christian light, and human reason to beleeve. And for such as can hardly beleeve that Melancholy, or distemper of body, and troubled phantasie, can cause people to imagine things so really, as to confess them to their own destruction, though most false and impossible; let them but consider the late example of a grave Minister about the Isle of Ely, who by a troubled phantasie was so deluded (or rather did so delude himself by weakness of Phantasie and imagination) as he reported that an Angel told him, that the Judgement Day should be upon the next Friday; by which report many of the Inhabitants were much troubled till the day was over; if then a grave Minister may be mis-led by Phantasie, and distempered minde; how much more plain common people, who have such Accusations brought against them as are sufficient to break their brains? Further I say, that if the man of sin spoken of in the second to the The Ssalonians, chap. 2. had not broached these errours to the world, these Confessors had had no such lying imaginations to confess, for their Confessions are not from themselves, but from the Devil, that so he might delude them that love not the truth, but do urge, and seek such Confessions against the truth, as it is said in the eleventh verse, For this cause. God shall send them strong delusions that they should beleeve, a lye, and c. Ninthly, Some will object, and say, They have helped search, and have sound Biggs, and privie Marks upon such as have been accused to be Witches; but I demand of them, Where doth the Scriptures teach us that a Witch is known by Biggs, or privie Marks? I also answer, That very few people in the World are without privie Marks upon their, bodies, as Moles or stains, even such as Witchmongers call The Devils privie Marks; which Marks Astrologians do affirm to be the characters of the Stars, variously fixed upon men according to their Nativity, and many an honest man or woman have such excrescences growing upon their bodies, as these Witchmongers do call, the Devils Biggs; as for example; There is a Disease often found in men or women in the seat of people, called Hemorroids, or Piles, or the swelling of the Hemorroids veins, a Disease well known to Physicians, many times swelling forth in the seat of people that are ful of Melancholy bloud, and are often found in fashion like Biggs, and sometimes issuing forth bloud, and for this Discase many have been accused by ignorant people, and put to death for Witches; this was part of the Evidence that was brought against Master Lewis a Minister, executed at Berry, in the year 1645. There are also found often times Excrescences upon the Bodies of men and women, called Verruca pensiles by the Physicians, as we may read in Leonartus Fuchsius, in the third Book of his Institutions of Pbysick, chap. 26. where he reckoneth up the several preter-natural tumors of mens Bodies; these are a certain kind of long fleshie Warts, in fashion of Biggs, or Teats, and do grow commonly on honest people, or any sort of people, and upon Beasts, and yet for these Excrescences being but outward tumors of the Body, many innocent people have been condemned and executed. Another Tumor is found by the Physicians, called Thymion both in Greek and Latine, rising on several parts of the body like Biggs, or Teats, these and other kindes of preternatural Tumors, of which we may read in Physick Authors, which sometimes being fell, and full of pain by reason of the rankness of bloud that feedeth them, and therefore issuing forth bloud, are called of ignorant Witchmongers, Devils Biggs. There be also some Natural parts of the Body called by a general name Glandule, and by a particular name Tonsilla, in the jaws of people, and in some people do plainly appear under the Tongue like little Biggs, which some ignorant Witchmongers having found in people, have taken them as a great evidence against poor innocent people, and for these have many been executed; but let any wise man consider, what body, of whatsoever constitution, especially of poor people that commonly want food, can spare a daily exhausting of bloud to nourish Imps sucking them, without an exhausting and over-throwing of their own Natural lives? whereas few poor or old people, but through want of nourishment and weakness of nature, have rather want of bloud, than an overpluss of bloud. There be also often found in Women with Childe, and in Women that do Nurse children with their Breasts, and in Women that by any accidental cause do want their menstruous courses, certain spots black and blew, as if they were pinched or beaten, which some common ignorant people call Fairy-nips, which notwithstanding do come from the causes aforesaid; and yet for these have many ignorant Searchers given Evidence against poor innocent people. But if any man will yet further cavil against Philosophy, and Physick Rules, then let him shew me any such description of a Witch in all the Scriptures, as Biggs, or Teats, or privie Marks, or Imps sucking them, or kept by them; and further I fay, that for any kinde of Biggs, or any things like Biggs, more than hath been found by Physicians to be preter-natural Tumors, or Diseases of the Body, or else Natural parts, to beleeve, is folly and madness, and to affirm, is a phantastick Lye, invented by the Devil, and the Pope. Tenthly, Some men will

Object, and say, If Witches have not power to affict, and torment, and kill People and Cattel, how cometh it to pass that after the angring of such an old man or woman, or such a lame man, or woman, that came to my House and desired relief, and I rated her away, and gave her no relief, or did not give her that which she desired; such and such crosses and losses came upon me, or such a Childe was taken in such a manner, with such a Sickness, presently after, or within fen days after his or her coming to my door? To this I answer, They that make this Objection must dwell very remote from Neighbours, or else must be known to give very little, or no relief to the poor, if it can be said at any time when a cross cometh upon them, that one poor body or other hath not been at their door that day, or not many days before, let it happen at any time whatsoever; shall this then be laid to the charge of him, or her that came last begging to their door? then by that reason no man in England can at any time be afflicted but he must accuse some poor body or other to have bewitched him; for Christ saith, The poor ye shall have always; and I think no man of ability is long free from poor coming to his door. Secondly, I answer, God hath given it as a strict Command to all men to relieve the poor, Levit. 25. 35. and in the next Chapter it followeth, vers. 14, 15. Whosoever hearkneth not to all the Commandements of the Lord to do them, (whereof relieving the poor is one) the Lord will send several crosses and afflictions, and diseases upon them, as followeth in the Chapter, and therefore men should look into the Scriptures, and search what sins bring afflictions from Gods hand, and not say presently, what old man or woman was last at my door, that I may hang him or her for a Witch; yea we should rather say, Because I did not relieve such a poor body that was lately at my door, but gave him harsh and bitter words, therefore God hath laid this affliction upon me, for God saith, Exod. 22. 23. 24. If thou any way affict widdows, and fatherless, and they at all cry unto me, I will surely hear their cry, and my wrath shall wax hot against thee. Thirdly, I answer, as Æsop faith in a Fable, Volunt homines ut plurimum quanáo suâ culpâ aliquid sibi acciderit adversi, infortunam vel dæmonem culpam canferre, ut se crimine exuant; and in his Moral he saith, Homines minime veniâ digni sunt qui cum liberèpeccent fortunam vel dæmonem accusant. So may I say of the most part of the World, who if by their own folly and negligence they wrong themselves; their Children, or their Cattel, they then accuse their Neighbour of Witchcraft, or if by their sins they bring down Gods Judgements, they then say they are bewitched, ascribing all to the Devil and Witches, never beholding Gods hand, or acknowledging that God is just, and themselves sinners. Eleventhly, Some wil stil object and say, What though there be no murthering, nor afflicting Witch mentioned in the Scripture, nor any command given to put Witches to death for Murthers, may not this common opinion of all men go for current, unless we can prove it by Scriptures? what shall one or two mens opinions be preferred before the common tenent of all men? To this I answer, It was the common tenent of all the Heathen, that Idols were gods, and ought to be worslnpped; it was the common opinion of all the Scribes and Pharisees that it was a sin to eat with unwashen hands, and yet the Scripture telleth us that these things were false. Secondly I answer, God gave his Laws, that we should add nothing to them, nor take any thing from them, Deut. 12. 32. why then should any man be so bold, contrary to the Commandement of God, to make it a Law to put poor people to death, upon foolish and feigned suppositions, or by the common tenent, and general blinde opinion of people without ground in the Scriptures? Twelfthly, Some will yet object and say, If we may not conclude Murthers and trials of Witches from Biggs and privie Marks, and sinking, and swimming in the water, because we have no warrant or mention of such trials in the Scriptures, then by the same consequence we may not try a Murtherer by any trial but such as is mentioned in the Scriptures; but this is taken for granted, that if a murthered man bleedeth new and fresh, when the Murtherer is near the dead Carcase, it discovereth the Murtherer, and many Murtherers have been discovered by Gods providence in that manner, and have confessed the Murther, and yet there is no warrant for this trial of a Murtherer in Scripture.

To this subtile Argument I answer, That a Judge may be too presumptuous in condemning a man upon any such evidence as that is; for a dead body will for the most part bleed fresh and new, if it lyeth two or three days unburied; as it is often seen in those that dye a natural death upon their Bed, and not Murthered, the bloud doth many times issue out of their mouthes in great abundance, at such times as the Humours of the body begin to putrife; and by the same reason a murthered Body will, when it hath lain two or three days, issue forth bloud, both at the mouth, and at the wound, whether the Murtherer be present or not. And what if God by his providence hath so brought it to pass sometimes, that the munthered body hath bled when the Murtherer hath been present, and so at the sight of the bloud the Murtherers Conscience hath so accused him that he hath been driven to confess the Murther? we may not thence conclude, or argue, that this is a certain trial of a Murtherer, without his own Confession, or other manifest proofs, for by that means we may sometimes condemn a guiltless man that standeth by at the same time of issuing forth bloud from the dead body, which is a common and a natural thing. Secondly, I answer this subtile Objection thus, Murther by the hand is a certain thing, we know it by experience, and also the Scripture speaketh of it, and for the trial and finding out of Murther, when we finde a man murthered, wee have an ordinance in the Scriptures, Deut. 21. the seven first verses, They were to make diligent inquisition according to the Law of Moses, and in the seventh verse every man ought to clear himself that his hand hath not shed the bloud of him that was slain; and if God blesseth his own ordinance of making such strict search and inquiry, by this wonderful and miraculous kinde of bleeding (as you suppose it to be) yet there is the ground of it, it is his own ordinance, and therefore God blesseth it, and discovereth the Murther; But now to apply this to a Witch, there is no consequence at all, for when we finde a man dead, or when any party is diseased, we have not any ordinance in the Scripture to make search who hath bewitched such a man, or killed such a man by Witchcraft, but whose hand hath slain him.

As also in Numb. 35. 16. who hath smitten him with an instrument of Iron, or any material instrument, or hand-weapon; wee may not then expect that God should answer mens fancies, and vain imaginations of Murthering by Witchcraft, that have no ordinance in Scripture, as he doth his own Ordinances; and for sinking, and swimming, Biggs and privie Marks, that may as well happen to one man as to another, to make them signs and trials of Witches, or Murtherers, is a groundless thing, and indeed at first invented by the Popes Inquisitors, who rather than they would not insnare whom they aimed at to put them to death, they would make any thing a sign or token of a Witch; and if all these signs that these Popish tyrants have affirmed to be signs, were as they say, true signs of Witches, then all people under the Heavens might be by one sign or other proved to be Witches; these signs may as well signifie a Thief, or a Cut-purse, as a Witch, being indeed no signs at all.

Thirteenthly, Some will object and say, If we may not suppose that Witches can kill, or afflict people by Witchcraft, except we have ground and warrant for it in the Scriptures, them by the same reason we may not hang a Thief for Felony, for by the Scriptures; he ought to have restored four-fold, and we finde no warrant in Scripture to put him to death? To this it is answered, to put a Thief to death for Theft, is either lawful, or unlawful; if it be not lawful by the Scriptures, though a thing commonly done, then we may not prove any thing lawful by instancing in a thing unlawful. Secondly, If it be lawful to put a Thief to death without warrant from the Scripture, as yee suppose it to be, yet therein we go beyond our warrant, only in the matter of punishment, which punishment yet falleth upon the guilty Thief, who is certainly convicted by infallible testimony, according to Gods ordinance; but whosoever putteth man or woman to death for bewitching people to death, or for afflicting man or beast with diseases by Witchcraft, goeth beyond his warrant in matter of guilt, for the Scripture no where saith that a Witch was, or can be guilty of any such thing as killing by Witchcraft, or afflicting by Diseases, or any cross or adversity by

Witchcraft upon men or cattel, and so in this we sin not, in inflicting greater punishment upon a Witch then is due by the Law of God (for by Law we ought not to suffer a Witch to live) but the sin is, in inflicting punishment upon the innocent, in Condemning them for Witches which are not Witches, for a Witch in the Scriptures is only a seducer of the people to Idolatry, and for killing without a stroak of the hand, or some material instrument, God claimeth it as his own Prerogative proper to himself only, Deut. 32. 39. I Sam. 2. 6 so that imputing it to any other, is against the Scriptures. Fourteenthly, Some will object and say, Although there were no Murtheing Witches spoken of in the Scriptures, or any such description of a Witch, as one that maketh a League with the Devil, or that lyeth with Incubus, or Succubus, or that hath Imps, or Biggs, or privie Marks by which they are known, yet such may be sprung up since the Scriptures were written, as new sins increase daily.

To this I answer, If there be new sins it must be in reference to the Law, for that maketh sin to be sin, because it is a breach of the Law; now, No man may adde any thing to the Law of God, Deut. 12. 32. and therefore we may not suppose that there be any sins that are not mentioned in the Law; also such sins are not mentioned in the Gospel; and Saint Paul saith, Whosoever preacheth any other Gospel than that we have received, let him be accursed, Gal. 1. 9. Fifteenthly, it hath been objected by some, That a Judge, or a Jury-man, is not to question any truth of opinion concerning the power of Witches, or what Witches are, but to be guided by the Law of the Nation, and to go according to the evidence of Witnesses, and if any one will come and witness upon Oath against any man or woman, that he or she is a Witch, the Jury ought to cast her, and the Judge ought to condemn her. To this Objection I answer, Deut. 17.6. At the mouth of two or three witnesses shall he that is worthy of death be put to death, but at the mauth of one witness he shall not be put to death. It is taken for granted, that a man or woman is sometimes given over to bear false witness, therefore God hath made it one of his Commandements, Thou shalt not bear false witxess; and here in Deut. 17.6. God hath given us this rule to avoyd false witness, That one Witness shall not pass as a sufficient evidence upon Life and Death, and yet many have wrongfully suffered death at the mouth of one Witness, contrary to this Law, without examination of the condition of the Witness, whether Mad, or foolishly presumptuous, or malicious. Secondly I answer, Where two or three Witnesses are to pass for true evidence against any Person, it is to be understood only in matters prescribed by the Word of God, as Murther by an instrument smitten, or cast at a person, or by the hand, or by some apparent infallible way, Numb. 35. 16, and c. but not in matters that are no way grounded upon the Word, but are flat contrary to the Word of God, and are only mens imaginations, for we have no warrant to put any person to death upon any imaginary offence (if it were likely that two or three should agree together in such a testimony) neither ought a Judge, or any Magistrate to administer an Oath, or take, or hear an Oath in any thing Moral that is not prescribed in Gods Word, but only imaginary; and if two or three would swear point blank against any person to be a Witch, they ought not to he suffered to swear against any in that manner, except it be to swear against such Witches as the Scripture speaketh of, according the whole discourse of this Book, and therein also they ought to give a reason of their Oath, and the Judge and Jury to consider it. Thirdly I answer, That Oathes that have been usually taken against many persons in that kinde, are not to be regarded, though true; as that such a one hath been seen to have a Rat or Mouse creep upon her, or under her Coats, or was heard talking to her Imps, these are not material testimonies, but are foolish and sensless arguments, not grounded in the Word of God. Further, if the Witnesses can swear that any person keepeth and feedeth Imps, it is not a material Oath, for it is as lawful to keep a Rat, or Mouse, or Dormouse, or any Creature tame, as to keep a tame Rabbit, or Bird; and one may be an Imp as well as another, and so may a Flea or Louse by the same reason; and so the Devil need not go far for a bodily shape to appear in, or to suck mens or womens flesh in; and if these were material Oathes, who then may not be proved a Witch? and yet there was an honest woman (so always formerly reputed) executed at Cambridge in the year 1645. for keeping a tame Frogge in a Box for sport and Phantasie, which Phantasie of keeping things tame of several species is both lawful and common among very innocent harmless people, as Mice, Dormice, Grashoppers, Caterpillers, Snakes; yea a Gentleman, to please his Phantasie in trying conclusions, did once keep in a Box a Maggot that came out of a Nut, till it grew to an incredible bigness; all these are Arguments of no force; yea I further say, if two or three would swear that they saw such a Creature suck any persons flesh, it doth not prove it to be a Devil, or that the Devil is in it, or therefore the Person a Witch. Lastly I answer, If a Judge, or a Jury be bound by the Law of the Nation to proceed according to that Law, yet they are bound more by the Law of God to proceed according to his Law, and if there be any Law of any Nation made to put to death people for any supposed imaginary Witchcraft, not spoken of in Gods Word, that Law ought to be abrogated, for we may not adde to Gods Law, Deut. 12. 32. and in the mean time, that Nation that maintaineth such a Law, that Judge, that Jury which prosecuteth such a Law (being not grounded in, but contrary to the Law of God) they all hazard themselves under the Curse of Gods Law, Exod. 22. 23, 24. Sixteenthly, The last and wisest Objection is this, It is maniest in the Scriptures that a Witch may kill by Witchcraft, for it appeareth Numb. 25.9. that after Balaam had tried all ways to Curse the people, there dyed of the people twenty four thousand, and although he could not hurt them by Inchantment (as he affirmeth chap. 23.23. There is no Inchantment against Israel) yet it appeareth, Revel. 23.14. that he taught Balac to lay a stumbling-block before the people, in inticing them to commit Idolatry, which brought down the anger of God upon them that they dyed, Numb. 25.9. To this I answer, This indeed is the only Witchcraft that can kill or hurt any man (according to the whole Discourse of the First Book, of this Treatise) seducing the people to Idolatry, whereby they do cause them to provoke God to anger, and to strike them in his displeasure; and this is the Doctrin we ought to learn by the History of Balaam, yea this is the only Witchcraft that is summarily included in all the Nine tearms of Description, Deut. 18. 10, 11. (being the discourse of my first Book) and to shew any proof of any sort of Witches in the Scriptures, I challenge all Witchmongers, yet some will forsake the Scriptures, and confute me strongly, with a repetition of some of Bodins lyes, or the like Stories, telling them for truth. But for all such as do still labour, by Objections, Cavils, Inventions, and Imaginations, to uphold the old Traditions and Errours of that grand Witch the Pope, and his Train, concerning Witches, and their Power, and not rather to cleanse the world from these Doctrins of Devils; let them take heed that the saying belongeth not to them, that Stephen spake to the Jews, Acts 7.51. Yee stif-necked and uncircumcised in heart and ears, yee do always resist the Holy Ghost, as your fathers did, so do yee; As it is written, 2 Thes. 2.10, 11,12. because yee received not the love of the truth, that yee might be saved; for this cause God hath sent you strong delusions, that you should beleeve a lye, that they all might be damned who beleeved not the truth, but had pleasure in unrighteousness. A Conclusion. He that groundeth his Opinion upon Phansie and Human traditions, and reports, without light, and rule of the Scriptures, is like a man groping in the dark, who for want of light rusheth his face against the door. But if any man will forsake blinde imaginations, and be guided by the light and rule of the Scriptures, he shall finde by them, that Witches are only false Prophets, who used several deluding impostures to deceive the people (according to the whole Discourse of the first Book of this Treatise, and these were not poor men and women, such as are commonly executed for that falsly-imputed Crime of Witchcraft) but were open practicers of their several Witchcrafts, to delude and seduce, and those had not their Craft from a Familiar, or by making a League with the Devil, as hath been commonly imagined, but were in a manner learned, and used Books written for that purpose, to teach them their manifold impostures, whereby to gain a maintenance among the people, by making them beleeve they were Prophets; as wee may read, Acts 19. 19. many of them being converted by the powerfull preaching of the Gospel, brought their Books, and burnt them before the people; these Books containing such subtile devices as were practised then by the false Prophets, or Witches of the time, to deceive the people, and now adays by the Popish Rout, and by our common Wizzards. But now for the thousands of people that have been executed for Witches in several parts of the World, by the common manner of fond, accusations, at whofe hands will God require their bloud, but at the hands of the Whore of Rome, and of those that have joyned with her in her abominations? Revel. 18. 24. In her was found the bloud (not only of Saints) but of all that were slain upon the earth. This doubtless must be understood of thofe that are unjustly slain, and who are they, but such as are slain by wrongful accusations? which wrongful accusations are occasioned by the devillish Doctrins wherewith she hath defiled the Nations. Further I say, That this Doctrin of Witches power is the main strength of Antichristian policy; for whereas that Romish Whore knoweth, that in all Nations the Civil Magistrate will hold his power, and not resign it to her, to have absolute power to kill for Religion, she maintaineth this damnable Doctrin to this end, that under the name of Witches she may melt away all whom she feareth, or suspecteth will be opposers of her Antichristian pride, and herein she ingageth the Civil Magistrate, by her subtill Doctrin, to cut off whom she pleaseth; and how can that be said to be a Government for the defence of peoples Lives and Estates? where contrary to all Law these Villains can steal away both life and estate from whom they please (except from such as are in places of Dignity, or so well esteemed in Common-wealths, or have such friendship among the potent of the Land, that thereby they are able to withstand their Adversaries) and these poor accused people have no redress, or help at the hands of the Magistrate; but he who ought to be their Defender is bewitched, and ingaged against them; he is taught indeed not to suffer a Witch to live, but never truly taught who, and what are Witches; and that many times they that ingage him by their lying Doctrin, are the very Witches themselves, aimed at in the Scriptures, that ought not to be suffered to live.

THE THIRD BOOK

SHEWING

The vanity of some English Writers concerning Witches. BOdinus, Hyperius, Hemingius, and other Popish Bloud-suckers, mentioned before in the Second Book of this little Treatise, having defiled the World with their abominable inventions, contrary to the sense and truth of Gods Word, their devillish Doctrins being already declared sufficiently to be wholly dissonant to the Word of God; yet some of our English Writers (who otherwise might seem to have been wise and learned men) have defiled their Pens with these groundless Phantastical Doctrins, which Writers are briefly these. The first is James Bishop of Winton, setting forth three Books, called Dæmonology, in the name and title of the Works of King James (and whether the Bishop or the King were the Composer of that Work, I stand not to argue) which Works are collected out of these Popish Writers before mentioned, which the Author acknowledgeth in the Preface to his Book, where he alledgeth Bodinus, Hyperius, and Hemingius for confirmation of the truth of the matter contained in his Works, but not a jot of Scripture is produced in all the Work, if rightly interpreted, to prove it to be truth, and yet the Author himself confesseth of Bodinus, that his Book of Dæmoxomanie is collected with greater diligence, than composed with judgment; and truly I wish every wise man (that desireth to be resolved in his judgement concerning these Opinions) to observe that passage; or if he be such a one as can read, and search the severall Writers of this subject of Witchcraft, let him observe the variety of their Opinions, how few of them do agree in one tenent, or in their manner of writing, by which it is easily concluded, that all their traditions are but Phantsies, contrary to the sound of Gods Word; even as a wise Judge, examining several Witnesses of one thing, if he findeth not their testimony to agree, he concludeth, that they compacted together to witness a thing false; and truly, although wise and learned men have been deluded by these lying inventions, yet compare but their Opinions one with another, and also with Holy Writ, and you shall finde, that all their Opinions are but one monstrous Devil, striving to get the mastery of the Spirit of truth; and whether this Work was either composed by King James, or by the Bishop, may be very well suspected, or rather by some Scotish man, blinded by some Scotish Mist, who desired to set forth his own Tenents for the upholding of Popish errours, and Popish Writers, sufficiently confuted before by Scot, in his Discovery of Witchcraft, he not being able any whit to answer Scot in his Discourse, laboureth to uphold false Tenents and Doctrins, by the authority of a King, because he could not finde any thing in the Scriptures to uphold them, or to answer Scot, as wee may read in the Preface, that his whole aime is at Scot, whom he falsly chargeth with the Tenent, and Affirmation, That there is no such thing as Witchcraft; whereas Scot in all his whole Book saith no such thing, but only that Witchcraft is a craft of deceiving, and seducing the people, and not of killing and making barren, and raising Winds, and such like Inventions; he that readeth that Preface, and seeth how Scot is first and chiefly aimed at in the whole Work, might presently expect that in the Work he should finde Scot notably confuted, or at the least in some way answered, but reading over the Work, he shall finde not one thing or other answered at all, but only a bare affirmation of such Tenents, without any ground, or warrant of the Scripture, which Tenents were confuted by Scot, by the Scriptures; so that for any man to answer that Work of the Author at large, were only to do that which Scot hath already done, in confuting Bodinus and others; and whereas this Author pretendeth a refutation of Scot, he hath done nothing else but written again the same Tenents that Bodinus and others had before written, and were by Scot confuted; like Argument, though never so foolish, he will deny the Conclusion. One Disputant wisely and plainly proveth that a thing is, and the other foolishly saith still it is not; or one proveth that a thing is not, and the other foolishly still saith it is; by which way of arguing a childe may hold an Argument against a learned Doctor, though never so false. Yet for the answering of the Tenents of this Author in that Work, First, he saith in his first Book, as also in the Preface, That Witches can by the help of the Devil cause to be brought unto them all kindes of dainty Dishes for their delicious maintenance; (and yet say I, how many poor lean starved people have been executed in several places for Witches) and for the truth of this Doctrin, he bringeth no place of Scripture to prove it, but only affirmeth it to bee true, for these reasons; First, The Devil is a Thief, and delighteth to steal. Secondly, He is a Spirit, and therefore can subtilly, and suddenly transport the same from whence and whither hee will; by which way of argument, rejecting the Scriptures, a man may affirm for truth any vain imagination, be it as absurd as this former; as, that the Devil is a Thief, and therefore hath a Mountain of Gold, which he hath taken out of every mans Purse, and heaped up in Hell, which he being a Spirit, hath easily transported from the earth, and therefore are so many men hastening to Hell, because there is abundance of Gold; But if such foolish Arguments as these were of any force, what need then any Scripture to teach us the truth? But if we examine the truth of this Doctrin by the Scriptures, it will prove for want of ground in Scripture very phantastical, and in opposition to the truth of the Scriptures very blasphemous; for hereby we should yeeld still that what was done by the Angel of God in miraculous manner, bringing food to Elijah, I King. 19. 6. may be done by the Devil, bringing variety of food to them that serve him; and whereas God by a Miraculous hand brought his people through a barren Wilderness, and fed them in that Wilderness; the same thing might as well have been done by the Devil, who (saith he) can bring his servants all manner of dainty dishes. This that is already written were enough to disable, and make voyd all the three Books of Dæmonologie written by this Author; but yet for the satisfaction of such as will expect a Methodical answer, I will begin with his Works in order as they stand, and in brief shew the vanity of them; as for example, he saith in his Epistle to the Reader, Sorcery and Witchcraft are different from Magick, and Necromancy, and yet

143

in the first Chapter of the Second Book, he saith, the Maid spoken of in the sixteenth of the Acts was a Witch, because she had the spirit of Python, and yet we finde in the Scripture, that they that had the spirit of Python, were also Necromancers; how then can this distinction hold, that Witchcraft differeth from Necromancy? for by that distinction a Pythonist were a Witch, and a Necromancer not a Witch; yet what was the Pythonist of Endor but a Necromancer, pretending to consult with the dead? and Necromancy was the pretence of all that were said to have the spirit of Python; that was, that they consulted with the Souls of the dead, as in Plutarch, and also in holy Writ, as in Isa. 8. 19. (it is manifest in any Tongue but our English) which in Tremellius translation is to this sense; for when they shall say unto you, Ask counsel of those that have the spirit of Python (or the imposture of Oracling) and of South-sayers, should not a people ask counsel of their God? Shall they ask counsel of the dead for them that are living? so then it is plain, this diftinction is wholly diffonant from Scripture, and that this Author wrote not according to Scripture, but by phantasy and imagination.

And now for his First Book, and the whole discourse of it, he layeth this foundation, he produceth these places of Scripture to prove that there is such a thing as Witchcraft and Witches, Exod. 22. 18. I Sam. 15. 23. Acts 8. Acts 16. and here he never searcheth the sense and meaning of these Scriptures, but proveth that Witches are, which thing no man denyeth; and yet mark but his proofs, Exod. 22. 18. which is taken for a Jugler, or one that worketh false Miracles to deceive and seduce, in the same sense is to be understood, Acts 8. 9, 10. concerning Simon Magus who was a Jugler and Magician (Jugling being one main part of Magick in the Scripture discourse) such were Pharaohs Magicians, which Magicians this Author, distinguisheth from Witches, and yet would prove by these places that there is such a thing as Witchcraft and Witches; so likewise I. Sam. 15. 23. Rebellion is as the sin of Divination, from hence hee would prove Witchcraft also, and yet his distinction denieth that Necromancers (whose main drift was to give Divinations, by consulting with the dead) are Witchess and this is the sum of his first Chapter, where any wise man may see how he hath lost himself in proving, and not able to prove that which is easily proved, and that which no man denieth, That there is such a thing as Witches and Witchcraft; for all the rest of his Discourse in his first Book, it is to prove that there are Magicians and Necromancers, which thing no man denieth according to the Scriptures; but though this be a true Conclusion, yet it ariseth not from his proofs before mentioned, according to his own distinctions, for he produceth those proofs only to prove that there are Witches, which yet he distinguisheth from Magicians and Necromancers; how vainly then doth he raise from these proofs a discourse of Magicians and Necromancers? And further, in all this Difcourse, he writing only according to his own imaginations, without grounds in the Scriptures, or in Arts, and Sciences, he runneth into gross absurdities, as in the third Chapter, that Judicial Astrologie is attained by Circles and Conjurations, raising of Spirits to resolve their doubts, which sheweth how little reading he had in that Science; and in the fourth Chapter he bringeth in healing by Charms, and Stones, and Herbs, as if by his method they were a part of Astrologie, and not only in that hath he shewed his weakness, but in reckoning Stones and Herbs among Magick Charms. In the Fifth Chapter he saith, Magicians conjure the Devil in a Circle, and if they miss the least circumstance, the Devil breaketh into the Circle, and carrieth quite away Body and Soul; and yet saith, a little before, in the same Chapter, that the Devil having prescribed that form of doing, that he may seem to be commanded thereby, will not pass the bounds of those injunctions (Circles). In the sixth Chapter he talketh, That they make a League with the Devil written with their bloud, and so learn of him to play Jugling Tricks, and Tricks upon the Cards and Dice (in which also he sheweth himself but a silly Gamester, in thinking such Tricks cannot be played without a League with the Devil) and yet by his distinctions, and by his whole Difcourse, he saith, these Magicians (though in league with the Devil) are no Witches, which is contrary to the general Tenent that ever was of his own Sect (that is, where such a League was made, it made a Witch) but to speak the truth, the ill coherence of the Writings of his, and all other Writers of that sort, sheweth, that they have no ground but Phantsy, and Fiction, for any league or transaction with the Devil, either by Magician or Witch (to use his own distinction (though senceless) either in Scripture, or Human reason guided by the Scripture, and this is the whole scope of his first Book. In the First Chapter of his Second Book he refuteth himself, and plainly confesseth (though dully) that all his former proofs of Scripture concerning Witches were to bee understood only of Magicians, and not of Witches; but saith he, Though that be true, yet the Law of God speaketh of Magicians, Inchanters, Diviners, Sorcerers, and Witches, and whatsoever of that kinde that consult with the Devil, but doth not say where the Law speaketh so, nor where such are said to consult with the Devil, but letteth it pass for granted which yet I will grant; thus farre the Law of God speaketh of Magicians, Inchanters, Diviners, and Sorcerers, but not of Witches distinct from these, for these were Witches in all the Scripture-sence, and Diviners were Magicians, and Magicians were Sorcerers, and Inchanters were Witches, and so were all the rest; but still mark how he laboureth to produce some proofs beyond all this, whereby he would make a Witch somewhat (he cannot tell what) distinct from Magicians, Diviners, Inchanters, and Necromancers; for saith he, the Maid that followed Paul crying, Acts 16. was a Witch, whose spirit of Divination was put to silence, saith he, and she was a Witch, because she did not raise the Devil, but hee spake by her tongue publickly, and privately, and that by her consent, and this is his ultimate proof of a Witch; which I grant; she was a Witch, but why distinct from the rest? what was she more than a Diviner? and the Scripture saith she had the spirit of Python, which was a spirit of lying Prophecie or Divination; and saith he, she was a Witch, because the Devil spake by her tongue, and that by her consent, as if he spake not by the tongue of all Diviners, Inchanters, Pythonists, South-sayers, Necromancers, and all false

Prophets, and that by their consent; she was a Witch saith he, because she raised not the Devil, but yet say other Writers of his Sect, they are Witches that raise the Devil, and she had been a Witch if she had raised the Devil; and he himself in his seventh Chapter saith, Devils are made commonly to appear by Witchcraft; from these grounds in Scripture, (which are all spoken of Deceivers, and false Prophets, according to the whole discourse of my first Book, which indeed were Witches in the Scripture-sense, though weakly discovered by this Author) he goeth on presumptuously in the second and third Chapters, to say that Witches are such as do compact with the Devil, and in great number meet in Houses, and Churches, and adore the Devil in Pulpits, and learn of him to do mischief, and do render account at their several meetings, what mischief they have done for his service, and to kisse his hinder parts for adoration, and this is all the scope of his second and third Chapters, without any tittle of proof from Scripture, but only confession of Condemned people (which is no proof) being contrary to Scripture and reason, and (all Circumstances considered) is no Confession; for as he dully argueth in his first Chapter, that because they are loath to confess without Torture, therefore they are guilty; we may argue the contrary, they therefore are not guilty, their Confession being extorted, which Confession yet he would argue to be true, because saith he, the Devil was worshipped among the Heathen, and gave Oracles, and Responses, and was honoured with bloudy Sacrifice, and gave Divinations by the intrals of Beasts; But although these things were done by Heathen people that worshipped Idols, and had Oracles, and Responses from their Idol Priests (which were the Witches, and false Prophets of the times) and in that fence might be said to worship the Devil, as in I Cor. 10. 19, 20. (because the Devil was in the Idols, or rather in their Priests, and so by them wrought delusions under the mask of Idols) yet what consequence is here, that because the Devil was in this sence worshipped publickly by Idolaters, that therefore he is now privately worshipped by the great Conventions and Assemblies of Witches? or where do we read in Scripture, that Witches were such as did meet to worship the Devil? they were indeed such as seduced people to worshipping of Idols, by the delusions of the Devil ruling in their hearts. And in the fourth Chapter he saith, that VVitches can be transported in the Air, by the Devils help, because Habbakkuk was transported by the Angel, in the History of Daniel Apocrypha, which if this were a true story Canonical, yet what absurdity is this, to equalize the Devils power with the power of God by his Angel? And what consequence is here? If the Angel did so transport, therefore the Devil doth transport; and yet this is the whole scope of his fourth Chapter. In the fifth Chapter his whole scope is, That Witches can make pictures of Wax, or Clay, and rost them, and so consume the party whom they intend, and can receive from the Devil stones and powders, and by them cast on can Cure diseases; that they can raise Storms and Tempests, and do many strange things, and that no man is sure to escape their Witchcraft, which as I have shewed in my second Book, are not only inventions and fictions of Antichrist, without ground in Scripture, but flat against Scripture, and the faith of Christians to beleeve. And whereas he saith further, The Devil can send Witches to poyson people, I answer, so he may teach any man else that will undertake it; for that is not any whit more essential to a Witch than to any other murthering-minded man or woman, no more than stabbing with a Knife or Dagger. The scope of the sixth Chapter is, That the Devil appears to Witches, and teacheth them to do mischief, but yet they have not power to hurt a Magistrate; but sure if Witchcraft consisted any whit in the Art of poysoning, why then is the Magistrate free? for certainly many Magistrates, yea Judges, and Kings themselves, have been poysoned; hath a Witch then less faculty in poysoning Magistrates then other men have had? why then is their Craft counted so dangerous? The scope of his seventh and last Chapter is, that Spirits did more commonly appear in time of Popery than now, and the reason there of he giveth before he proveth it to be true; that is, that the Gospel hath dispelled those Spirits that were wont to appear. This reason hath a smooth pretence if it were given of a true thing, but the thing which he argueth upon is not true, for there were no more Spirits seen in time of Popery than now (and that is just none at all) but there were more lyes reported by papists, and in time of Popish ignorance, than now, and the Gospel indeed hath dispelled those Popish Errours which were wont to deceive the people morethan now; and who so denyeth that Spirits appear, he saith they are Sadduces, whereas yet there was never any such dispute among Sadduces, whether Spirits did appear visible or not; neither were the Pharisees that opposed the Sadduces so silly as to affirm any such thing; but if any such thing were, as visible apparition of Spirits, doubtless it had been no Controversie, for the Sadduces might have seen them as well as the Pharisees; this is the scope of his First and Second Book. And here I am compelled to go back again to the third Chapter of the First Book, to answer one of his Tenents, which I think very material to be answered out of order, because if I had taken it in order it would have spoyled my method in answering so curtly as I have done, (his writing being somewhat immethodical.) Look in his first Book, the third Chapter, and see how he by the bare signification of a word, laboureth to ground an absurdity, saying, Necromancy is one that Prophesieth by the dead, and that is, saith he, one that consulteth with the Devil, assuming the body of the dead party; but as I have said, what Logician doth not know that it is not a legal manner of arguing, but most absurd to draw a Conclusion from the bare signification of words, or from what words may signifie? but he that argueth truly, must argue as the words are taken, and not as they may signifie, and also search the Original sence of the Hebrew, and yet for the word it self it hath not the least signification of the Devil, or that the Devil can assume a dead Body, or the least signification of Prophecying by the Devil, but only by the dead, according to the vain Tenent of the Heathen, that the Souls of the dead (by reason of their perfect estate after this life) could inspire men living upon the earth, with knowledge of things to come, in which pretence these Witches called Necromancers used Divinations, or lying Prophecies, as manifestly appeareth in Plutarch, de. defect. Orac. and by Scripture, as I have showed

149

more fully in the Ninth description in my first Book; and as for that Tenent, that the Devil can assume and raise a dead Body, it is most absurd and blasphemous, for it was by the divine miraculous power of Christ upon the Cross, that the bodies of the dead were raised for a time, and appeared unto many, Matth. 27. 52, 53. from whence the Centurion acknowledged Christ to be the Son of God, knowing, that such things could not be done but by the mighty Power of God; yet if this absurdity were true, That the Devil could assume the bodies of the dead, it makes nothing to prove their common main Tenent, that Witches are such people as can kill by Witchcraft, for a Necromancer is only one that taketh in hand to Prophesie by the dead, or to give divinations, and not one that killeth, or witcheth people to death; neither doth it agree with this Authors distinctions to hold any such Tenent, that a Necromancer is one that consulteth with the Devil assuming a dead body, for he saith in his Sixth Chapter of his Second Book, and also in the third Chapter of the Third Book, that the Devil appeareth to Witches, and they consult with him, having assumed a dead body; why then doth he in his former distinctions make a difference betwixt a Necromaucer and a Witch? And now to proceed to the Third Book, as followeth, He laboureth to prove in his Third Book, That the Devil can appear bodily, and doth commonly haunt Houses and Fields in shape of men departed this life, and sometimes as Fairies, sometime in manner of Browning (as he calleth it) that is it that by our old Wives Fables is called Robin Good-fellow) and that these are true, and not false Fables, and for that in his first Chapter he allegeth, Isa. 13. 21. where it is said, That Zim and Ohim shall dwell in their houses, and Jim shall cry in their Palaces, which saith he, are in the Hebrew the proper names of Devils; but how erroneous this exposition is, let them that can read the Hebrew text see, and for them that cannot read the Hebrew text, let them read the Latine translation of Junius and Tremellius, which is thus; Et recubabunt seræ illic, and implebunt domos eorum noxia animalia; habitabuntq; illic ulule, and scopes saltabunt illic, clamitabitq; terrificum animal in viduatis palatiis ipsius, and serpens in templis voluptariis: That is, Wilde Beasts shall lodge there, and hurtful Beasts shall fill their Houses, and Owls shall dwell there, and Night-birds shall hop there, and a Dragon shall cry in their desolate Palaces, and the Serpent in their pleasant Temples; (Tremellius in his Marginal Notes saith, Terrificum animal, id est draco) Those were all only such Creatures as do commonly inhabit desolate places; The Prophet speaking in the former verse of desolation that should come upon the Land; and indeed the Devil hath least to do in desolate places, and is most busied where people are most; but had Zim and Tim been the proper names of Devils, it had not made any thing to the purpose, to prove that the Devil walketh up and down in corporal appearance, for it is said, Revel. 2. 13. that the Devil dwelt at Pergamus, and yet it is not meant that he was there seen at all to appear in any shape, but was there in the hearts and works of wicked men, but such is the manner of all that are tainted with Popish Tenents, that they would have people conceive of the Devil, that he is some ugly terrible Creature to look upon, some black man with a pair of Horns on his head, and a Cloven Foot, and along Tayl, or some monstrous Beast that inhabiteth in Woods, and walketh about in the night to scare people, and this doctrin is maintained by Popish Writers, least people should discern that the Devil is in all their Popish Doctrins and actions, and in the hearts of all Popish seducers, and deceivers of the world. Further, in this his Third Book he talketh of Incubus, and Succubus, as if it were an undoubted truth that the Devil lyeth commonly with Witches of both Sexes, having copulation with them, but for this he hath not the least Scripture, nor the least seeming Argument, but only constrained, extorted, belyed, nullified Confession of poor condemned people, which is the only Argument for all the devillish Tenents of all Writers of this sort, and yet they begin with Scripture, saying, Thous shalt not suffer a Witch to live, and upon this they raise a long discourse, contrary to all Scripture, and truth, and possibility, all which they will father upon the Scriptures, and yet when they are pinched by dispute to prove their Tenents by Scripture, they fly off to confe ssion; this confession I say is in all the discourse of this Author his only Argument (which is no Argument) and yet he pretendeth his discourse to be grounded on the Scriptures, and in that pretence in his last Chapter he concludeth his whole discourse with the Law of God, saying, Therefore these people ought to be put to death according to the Law of God, whereas yet in all his discourse he could not produce the least jot or tittle of the Law against any such kinde of supposed Witches as he talketh of nor the least colour of argument to prove his supposals, in all the Law, or all the Scriptures, without misconstruing the Law of God, and the Scriptures, So much for this Author. Cooper answered. THe second English Writer upon this subject is one Thomas Cooper a Minister, who himself being infected with the common Popish tenent, sent forth by Pope Innocent the Eighth, and Pope Julius the Second, and affirmed by Bodinus, and other bloudy Inquisitors mentioned in my Second Book, that Witches are Murtherers, and such as can raise Winds, and do things impossible, by the help of the Devil; This Cooper, instead of being himself a Minister to instruct, and teach the people in Gods Truth, grounded in Scriptures, he became a bloudy Inquisitor to finde out Witches, that is a bloudy Persecutor of the poor, and an accuser of them to be Witches, who by his blinde zeal in this kinde did cause many to be executed for Witches, as he confesseth in his first Book, the first Chapter, and sixteenth Page, and after this he reading Mr. Scots Discovery of Witchcraft, which he was no way able to confute by Scripture, nor to answer him truly, hee being galled in his Conscience, and netled in his minde concerning his reputation in the World (which he feared he should loose if his wickedness should be convicted and laid open) instead of humbling his Soul before God, and begging pardon for his sin; he wrot a Book in defence of his errours, called the mystey of Witchcraft, wherein he hath (as others have done) pretended to confute Scot, and to that end hath writ down many Popish inventions, adding thereunto many of his own foolish imaginations, without one jot of Scripture to prove or ground any of his Tenents, and after long discourse of meer Iyes and imaginations, in a pretence of holy Zeal, yet quite contrary to Gods truth (yea I may say, imaginations resisting Gods holy Spirit of Truth) bath thought it a sufficient confutation of Scot, to fetch him over with an use of reproof, as appeareth in his first Book, the eighteenth page, just as if a man should preach contrary to the Scriptures that Idols are gods, and labour to prove it by experience (as this Cooper laboureth to prove his Tenents concerning Witches) or to prove it by the example of such as have been slain, because they would not fall down before an Idol, and worship it (as this Cooper laboureth to prove his errours concerning Witches from the example of many that have been executed for Witches) and then should fetch them over with an use of reproof, that say Idols are no gods; and after this groundless use of reproof, this Cooper goeth on still in a frivolous discourse, without any Scripture to prove his Doctrin, and at last laboureth to shew that Juglers are Witches, which no man yet did ever deny (if they were such as wrought false Miracles to seduce the people, as Jannes and Jambres, and Simon Magus, and Elimas the Sorcerer) but he laboureth to prove that common Juglers are Witches, that do work their Tricks of Activity, saith he, by a Familiar, which yet (saith he) are no real Miracles, but they hurt the Eye, and thicken the Air, saith he, whereby they make things seem to be really done that are not done; which thing for a Jugler to do, that is, to hurt the eye, and touch it not, and to thicken the Air were a Miracle it self; but to clear these vain Fancies, who knoweth not that Juglers do play their Tricks only by the slight of hand, called Cleanly Conveyance, or Legerdemain ? and what common Jugler that hath gone about to Fairs, or Markets, to shew his Tricks of Activity to get Mony, will not in private for a shilling shew any Trick that he hath acted openly, and shew how it is done to the satisfaction of any man that desireth it, and that without a Familiar, or the least appearance of any such vain Phantsy as fools imagine; But yet if I should take it for granted, that these common Juglers are Witches, and do work their Feats by a Familiar Devil, as he affirmeth, yet what doth that make towards the proving of these poor, and aged, and lame people to be Witches, that have so commonly been said to be Witches? What Tricks of Activity have they shewed, either in Fayers or Markets, or in publick, or in private? surely if they had been Condemned for Witches, for any such thing doing, they should not need to be found out by an Inquisitor, to be tried by Biggs, or privie Marks, or by sinking or swimming in the water, for their actions would declare them openly. Also if common Juglers were Witches, as he saith; yet how doth this prove that a Witch is a Murtherer, which is the main drift of his Book; and to that end he bringeth many places of Scripture to prove that, there are Witches, which thing no man doth deny. Afterward he affirmeth, that Witches do make a real League with the Devil, (which hath been a common foolish tradirion) and for that he alledgeth Psal. 58. 5 where saith he the Original yeeldeth thus, Which heareth not the Charmer, or mutterer, joyning societies together, where (saith he) the Holy Ghost setteth down the effect of a Charm, namely, that it is able to stay the Adder from stinging those that shall touch him, but mark how this fellow belyeth the Scriptures, for which (because many understand not the Hebrew) I referre them to the Translation of Iunius and Tremellius, which is this; Qua non auscseltat voci mussitantium, utentis incantation bus peritissimi, which hearkeneth not to the voyce of mutterers, or of the most skilful user of Charms, so that there is not a word of Joyning Societies to gether, not a word of the Devil, not of any league with the Devil; yet if it had been so, and that he could have proved such a League or Covenant, it had made nothing to prove that a Witch is a Murtherer (which is his drift) for a League might be made for a Deceiver, as well as for a Murtherer; And whereas he saith the place aforesaid proveth the effect of a Charm, that it can stay the Adder from stinging, it proveth the clean contrary; for if the Propher had said the Adder hearkneth to, or regardeth the voyce of a Charmer, it had proved that a Charm is effectual; but in that he saith the Adder regardeth not, or hearkneth not to the voyce of the Charmer be he never so skilful, it proveth that a Charm is of no force; and indeed the

Prophet doth there allude deridingly to the vanity of that Idolatrous conceit of the Heathen, who thought that charms had vertue in them, and so were seduced by charms to put confidence in charms and conjurations, according to the Sixth term of description in the First Book of this Treatise, shewing the common conceit of the Heathen concerning charms, appearing in their Poets; Frigidus in pratis; santande rumpltur unguis. This fellow doth further contradict himself sundry ways, one of his most manifest absurd contradictions is in page 85, where he confesseth that God only hath power to send Satan to torment the wicked, and afflict the godly, and yet he affirmeth in page 261, that Witches also can send Satan to possess men, and torment them. Who so pleaseth to read over this Author, shal find that he is bold to affirm, not only that the Devil doth at the command of a Witch raise storms, poy son the Air, blast Corn, kill Cattel, torment the bodies of men, but also cast out Devils, as in page 158, also that he sometimes enliveneth a dead childe, and bringeth it to a Witch in her travelling to bring forth childe, and telleth her that it is the childe born of her body, begotten by himself, and so, saith he, she is deceived with her new darling, as in pag. 122. so that according to the Devilish doctrin of this Author, the Devil can raise the dead, as Christ raised Lazarus and Dorcas, and cast out Devils, as Christ did; but to conclude, they that shall read his blasphemous and vain imaginations, and yet shall see there with all the pretence of holy zeal in all his Discourse, may plainly behold in him the Devil turning himself into an Angel of Light to deceive the World. And so I leave this Cooper where I found him, namely, in a Stationers shop, dear of taking up. Master Perkins answered. THere is yet another Author writing upon this subject of Witchcraft, wel known to all, and that is M. Perkins, who because he was such a chosen instrument of preaching, Gods Word in his life, I blush to name him, least some should think I go about to defame him so long after his death, whom I honor in his Grave; but yet to take away all suspisons in that kinde, let every one know, that the Volume of Mr. Perkins his Works, in which is contained that Treatise of

Witchcraft, was not put in print by himself, but were certain Writings found in his Study after his death, most of which were taught by him in the Pulpit in his Life-time, but not depth of Melancholly, or distempered brain, as I have formerly demonstrated in my Second Book, and therefore need no further answer. So much for this Author who I beleeve had more of the Spirit of truth in him than many of his profession. Now for all that have written in that kinde, I summon all Witch-mongers to shew me in the Old or New Testament, which are given as a rule of truth, the least inference of any such Doctrin as is delivered by them. Also, I desire any man of right understanding, to compare them with the Scriptures, and so compare also this my Book with the Scriptures, and to see which of them is most consonant with the Scriptures, and which is most dissonant from the Scriptures, and so to try them by Gods touch-stone of truth. The Conclusion, TO conclude, you that are convicted of your Errors, and yet do make a light matter of it, and lay it not to heart, was Cain and Ahab accursed for murthering of each of them one man, and do yee make it a light matter to have murthered thousands by your ignorant doctrin? What will it avail at the latter day, that yee have preached, and prayed, and spread forth your hands, and made great stir in pretence of Religion? If Christ shall say, Depart from me yee workers of iniquity, and shedders of innocent bloud? if thousands that are wrongfully slain shall rise up in Judgement against you, if it shall be said to many Ministers, and Preachers of the Word, in that yee have not taught against these abominations, yee are partakers in them. Causes of up holding the damnable Doctrin of Witches power.

IF I did not aime at brevity, I might enlarge this Volume upon these particulars following, which I will only name and leave them, being the causes of upholding the opinion of Witches power. Some Ministers for want of due examining of the Scriptures, have taught in the Pulpits unwarily, and inconsiderately, the Doctrin of Witches Power, as also some have published their Works in print.

2 Many Ministers although they are of the contrary opinion, yet have neglected to beat down the common phantastical conceit of people concerning Witches power.

3 The common hatred that all men do bear to a Witch, so that if any poor Creature hath the report of being a Witch, they joyn their hand with the rest in persecuting, blindly, without due consideration.

4 The salfe reports that are commonly raised in that kinde concerning Witches, whereby men lead one another like wandring lost Sheep, to beleeve lyes; it is certain it was done in such a place, I have credibly heard it.

5 Vain credulity, which all men are naturally prone unto ever since Adams Fall, that is a Vice whereby men are subject to beleeve every lying report, being the ground of infidelity; Credula mens hominis and erect a fabulis aures.

6 Infidelity, or not beleeving the Scriptures to be the only perfect rule of righteousness, and touch-stone of truth.

7 Ignorance of the Scriptures, either by wresting them, or by neglecting to search them, or want of being able to read them, or when they are read, want of ability to understand them; all such men may be led away with any opinion.

8 Generality of opinion maketh weak people, and ignorant to argue, sure it is safest to say, and think as others do.

9 Obstinacy in opinion in such as have some weak knowledge, let such be beaten from one Argument they will fly to another, and beat them from all Arguments, yet at last they will still hold their opinion.

10 Melancholly, which frameth much representation in the minde of any terrible report or doctrin (though it bee groundless and false) and causeth it to take great impression in the deluded understanding.

11 Timerousness, whereby men like little Children, and Women especially, are afraid of every idle fantastical report that they hear of Witches power, especially if they be alone in the dark.

12 Crackt Phantasie, whereby many a man or woman, specially in Sickness have strange Apparitions either in bed, or abroad, which they report to silly people, and are beleeved, whereas it is nothing but their broken and hurt fancy, occasioned in some by sickness or distemper, in some by much Drunkenness, in some by a blow on the head, and in Scholars sometimes by over-much study, whereby they presently conceit, and are judged by others to be bewitched, or at least to be pursued by a Witch, or by a Witches Imps, and judge so themselves.

13 People that are handled by strange Diseases, as Children in Convulsion Fits, or Women in Fits of the Mother, and the like, are by ignorant beholders; and sometimes by ignorant Physitians said to be bewitched, as were Frogmortens Children said to be falsely.

14 Old Wives Fables, who sit talking, and chatting of many false old Stories of Witches, and Fairies, and Robin Good-fellow, and walking Spirits, and the Dead walking again; all which lying fancies people are more naturally inclined to listen after than to the Scriptures.

15 Another abominable cause is the suffering of Impostors to live, such as silly people call Cunning men, who will undertake to tell them who hath bewitched them, who, and which of their Neighbours it was, by the delusions of such Impostors, many poor innocent people are branded with a report of being Witches, by reason of which report coming first from a Witch, they are in process of time suspected, accused, arreigned, and hanged. A Reference to Mr. Scots Treatise of Spirits, and also the Opinion of Luther concerning Devils.

I Might further enlarge this Volume with a Treatise of Spirits, or the nature of Devils, concerning which people have much abused themselves for want of knowledge in the Scriptures, but for brevity I refer the Reader to Mr. Scot, who hath excellently written in the latter end of his Discovery of Witchcraft, a Discourse called, A Treatise of Spirits; also I thought good to adde in brief the words of Luther concerning Devils, which are these;

De phreneticis sic sentio, omnes moriones and qui usu rationis privantur à dæmonibus vexari, non quod ideo damnati sunt, sed quod variis modis Satan homines tentat, alios gravius, alios lenius, alios longius, quod medici multa ajusmodi trihuunt naturalibus causis, and remediis aliquando mitigant, fit quodignorant quanta sit potentia and jus dæmonum. Christus non dubitat, curvam illam anum in Evangelio, vinctam a Satana dicere; and Petrus Actorum decimo, oppressos a Diabolo dicit, quos Christus sanarat, ita etiam mulios surdos, claudos malitia Satana tales esse, Deo tamen premittente; deniq; pestes, febres, atq; alios graves morbos opera dæmoniorum esse, qui and tempestates incendia frugum calamitates operantur vere affirmamus; Summa mali sunt Angeli, quid mirum, si omnia faciunt mala humano generi noxia and pericula intentent, quatinus Deus premittit; etiamsi plurima talia herbis, and aliis remediis naturalibus curari possunt, volente Deo, and miserente nostri, exemplum Jobi endicat, quæ passus sit a Satana, quæ medicus omnia naturaliter fieri, and curari assereret; sciendum est igitur phreneticos a Satana tentari saltem temporaliter, an Satan non faceret phreneticos? qui corda replet fornicatione, c de, rapina, and omnibus, pravis affectibus; summa, Satan proprior nobis est quam ullus credere possit, cum sanctissinsis sit propinquissimus adeo, ut ipsum Paulum colaphizare and Christum vehere possit quorsum libet.

These are the words of Luther, and where he saith at the last, that the Devil could carry Christ whither he listed, it is his errour, for the Devil did not carry him at all, but led him by temptation, as appeareth, Luke 4. and as I have more at large written in my Second Book, in my answer to the Sixth Objection, if you look back to it; yet from this brief Discourse of Luther may be observed, That the Devil may be said to be an instrument in all

Diseases, crosses, and calamities, as Luther proveth by the Story of Job, and the saying of Christ concerning the woman, Luke 13. 11. 16. and as is expressed, 2 Thess. 2. 18. Luke 11. 14. but yet it must necessarily be true that the Devil is Gods Instrument in all these afflictions, as Job acknowledgeth in all his afflictions, ascribing all to God, Chap. 1. 22. 2. 10. 9. 34. and God claimeth these things as his own Prerogatives, Lev. 26. Deut. 32. 39.

From all which it is fully concluded, That the Devil is only Gods instrument to afflict and tempt the righteous, to afflict, tempt, and torment the wicked, and in all this doth nothing but by Gods peculiar dispensation, not by a bare permission, nor by the appointment of a Witch; whatsoever some have written more concerning the nature of Devils, as that there are Incubus, and Succubus, the He Devil, and the Shee Devil, that the Devil maketh a League with Witches, and that the Devil is the Witches Instrument as well as Gods, and that by Gods permission; that the Devil walketh in Church-yards, and near Sepulchers, and in desolate places; that he is black, that he assumeth a Corporal shape, that hee hath a Cloven Foot, that he walketh in the dark Nights, that he sometime roareth, and maketh a fearful noyse, that he useth to scare people in Woods and Fields, that there are fiery, aiery, earthy, and watery Devils, that there are degrees, orders, and supremacies among Devils, that some are greater in power than others; these are all dissonant to Scripture, and are only the vain fancies of men, who delight to fill the world with Fables. And whereas some do argue from Matthew 12. 24. that some Devils are greater in power than others, and also in degree and superiority, because Beelzebub is there called, The Prince of Devils, it is to be understood that the Pharisees called him the Prince of Devils, because Baal-zebub was the chief Idol by which the Israelites had been defiled sometimes, and was by them called therefore, the chief Devil, or the Prince of Devils, and was called by them Beelzebub, by an Antithisis, putting e for a, which Idol was spoken of, I Kings, I. 2. and Beza and Tremellius do both agree in that Exposition, that it is meant of Baalzebub, if we look their Notes upon Matthew 10. 25. and Beelzebub may bee interpreted, The Prince of Flies, not because Devils are Flies (as some imagine in the Story of Francis Spirah) but because his Temple was pestered with Flies, through the smell of the abundance of Flesh that was there spent daily, and also because the Country being much troubled with Flies, the people used to seek to that Idol for help against that annoyance of Fries, saith Beza.

Lucifer is also by some thought to be the chief among Devils, and that when he fell all his Angels fell with him, from that place in Isa. 14. 12, 13, 14, 15. but that is only an Allegorical exposition of the fall and exile of Nebuchadnezzar, who is there Metaphorically called Lucifer, because of his pride, in exalting himself as farre above others in his own thought, as the bright Morning Star exceedeth other Stars. He that would read these things more at large handled, may read Mr. Scot aforesaid, as also a little Book, called, The Deacon of Spirits. An Instruction for Lawyers. YOu that are learned in the Laws of the Land, are commonly found to be the most able and worthy to be Judges of the people, and these Laws which are the rule of Justice, are concluded by you, all to be exceeding good Laws; and therefore it must needs follow that such opinions as do make these Laws of no validity are absurd opinions, therefore I am bold to state two Questions, or Cases, and leave them to your Wisdoms:

> I. A man is found dead in the Fields, who a little before went out well; another man being his Adversary is questioned for his Life, as being suspected to have murthered him; this man proving that he was a hundred, or two hundred miles from the place where and when the man dyed, is quit by the Law. I demand then, what Justice is in that Law that quiteth him, if he might send the Devil, or leave order with the Devil or with his Imps, to Witch him to death at that time?

> II. Two men strive together, one overcometh and beateth the other, who presently sickneth, and within three days dyeth; the other is questioned by the Law for his Life; what Justice were in this Law, if an old Witch hating one,

or both of them, and seeing opportunity should have power to witch the one to death, that so the might cause the other to be Hanged for him?

FINIS.

Printed in Great Britain
by Amazon

46395867R00096